New Directions for Adult and Continuing Education

Susan Imel
Jovita M. Ross-Gordon
COEDITORS-IN-CHIEF

D0721774

Artistic Ways of Knowing

Expanded Opportunities for Teaching and Learning

Randee Lipson Lawrence
EDITOR

Number 107 • Fall 2005
Jossey-Bass
San Francisco

ARTISTIC WAYS OF KNOWING:
EXPANDED OPPORTUNITIES FOR TEACHING AND LEARNING
Randee Lipson Lawrence (ed.)
New Directions for Adult and Continuing Education, no. 107
Susan Imel, Jovita M. Ross-Gordon, Coeditors-in-Chief

Microfilm copies of issues and articles are available in 16mm and 35mm, as well as microfiche in 105mm, through University Microfilms Inc., 300 North Zeeb Road, Ann Arbor, Michigan 48106-1346.

NEW DIRECTIONS FOR ADULT AND CONTINUING EDUCATION (ISSN 1052-2891, electronic ISSN 1536-0717) is part of The Jossey-Bass Higher and Adult Education Series and is published quarterly by Wiley Subscription Services, Inc., A Wiley Company, at Jossey-Bass, 989 Market Street, San Francisco, California 94103-1741. Periodicals Postage Paid at San Francisco, California, and at additional mailing offices. POSTMASTER: Send address changes to New Directions for Adult and Continuing Education, Jossey-Bass, 989 Market Street, San Francisco, California 94103-1741.

SUBSCRIPTIONS cost $80.00 for individuals and $170.00 for institutions, agencies, and libraries.

EDITORIAL CORRESPONDENCE should be sent to the Coeditors-in-Chief, Susan Imel, ERIC/ACVE, 1900 Kenny Road, Columbus, Ohio 43210-1090. e-mail: imel.l@osu.edu, or Jovita M. Ross-Gordon, Southwest Texas State University, EAPS Dept., 601 University Drive, San Marcos, TX 78666.

Cover photograph by Jack Hollingsworth@Photodisc

www.josseybass.com

CONTENTS

EDITOR'S NOTES

In Lewis Carroll's *Alice's Adventures in Wonderland,* Alice contemplates how to get through a very small passage: "'Oh, how I wish I could shut up like a telescope! I think I could, if I only knew how to begin.' For you see, so many out-of-the-way things had happened lately that Alice had begun to think that very few things indeed were really impossible" (Carroll, 1960, p. 21).

The arts have always had the power to intrigue and capture the attention of many of us, yet they still remain on the margin of most educational programs, often relying on "soft money" for their survival. This volume demystifies the experience of art making and makes a strong case for the arts as an integral part of adult education. Art is seen as a way of knowing (Allen, 1995) that releases the imagination (Greene, 1995), allowing creative learning to emerge. Art appeals universally to us all and has the capacity to bridge cultural differences. Art can also foster individual and social transformation, promoting dialogue and deepening awareness of self and the world around us. Some of the authors in this volume also see art as a vehicle for promoting emancipation and social justice.

This volume challenges the dominant paradigm of how knowledge is typically constructed and shared in adult education settings by focusing on how adult educators can expand learning opportunities and experiences (for their learners), as Alice has shown is possible. The contributors to this volume are actors, musicians, photographers, storytellers, and poets, all of whom also happen to be adult educators. In each chapter, the author describes how one or more forms of artistic expression were used to promote learning in formal or informal adult education settings. In each case, the purpose of education was not to teach art (not to develop expertise in acting or poetry writing, or create great works of art). By contrast, art was used as a means to access learning in subjects as divergent as English language acquisition, action research, community awareness, and social justice.

Serving as an introduction to the volume, the first chapter begins with a discussion of the limitations of how knowledge has been traditionally constructed in adult education contexts and offers new creative venues for teaching and learning. The arts are depicted as a form of indigenous knowledge that is often present but buried within us. The benefits of art for teaching and learning in a variety of contexts are discussed. Each subsequent chapter focuses on an art form in a particular adult education context. The authors describe how they have incorporated artistic ways of knowing into their practice on the basis of their own and others' research.

Chapters Two and Three are situated in higher education. In Chapter Two, Kristin Lems talks about her experiences bringing music into an adult English as a second language class. Music is the tool that unlocks learning potential for adults from a variety of cultural backgrounds learning to speak

English. Chapter Three is situated in a cohort-based graduate program for practicing teachers. Anne McCrary Sullivan guides her students in creating poems to deepen their understanding of research skills. She also discusses her use of poetry as a volunteer interpreter at Everglades National Park and provides examples of her own poems as catalyst.

Chapters Four through Seven focus on the arts in community-based education. In Chapter Four, Keith B. Armstrong describes a technique combining photography with autobiography. The participants of a residential community took photos, wrote about their lives, and shared them in a group context. According to the author, "art is a record of social interaction and inevitable power relationships." People saw themselves in others' work, and their dialogue led to greater understanding. In Chapter Five, Steven E. Noble talks about the popular theater experience he created with adults battling mental illness. Art became a way for these marginalized adults to come out of the closet and face the world. Through their performance, they educated the community about the myths and realities of mental illness.

Chapter Six, by Kevin Olson, takes a look at the role of music in building communities both historically and today, from the Chautauqua, civil rights movement, and early folk schools to powwows and other ethnic festivals and modern-day youth centers, senior centers, and social action groups. The power of music to emancipate and promote group solidarity is emphasized. In Chapter Seven, Bette Halperin Donoho takes an in-depth look at an urban community performance group where community members act out stories focusing on problem solving and bringing about social change.

Chapter Eight weaves together the themes and threads of the previous chapters and strengthens the case for incorporating the arts into adult education. It is our hope through this volume that readers will be moved to pick up a paintbrush or a lyric pen, or express themselves through their whole body. After all, as Alice knows, very few things are really impossible.

Randee Lipson Lawrence
Editor

References

Allen, P. B. *Art Is a Way of Knowing*. Boston: Shambhala, 1995.

Carroll, L. *Alice's Adventures in Wonderland* and *Through the Looking Glass*. New York: New American Library of World Literature, 1960. (Originally published in 1865 and 1872)

Greene, M. *Releasing the Imagination*. San Francisco: Jossey-Bass, 1995.

Randee Lipson Lawrence is an associate professor in the department of Adult, Continuing, and Literacy Education at National-Louis University.

1

Traditional forms of teaching and learning based on textual forms of representation and rational thought may limit how we perceive our world. Artistic forms of expression and their implications for adult education are discussed.

Knowledge Construction as Contested Terrain: Adult Learning Through Artistic Expression

Randee Lipson Lawrence

On a recent trip to Santa Fe, I took the opportunity to visit the Awakenings Museum. It features just one exhibit, an eleven-thousand-square-foot space covered floor to ceiling with the work of the French painter Jean-Claude Gaugy. The exhibit depicts Gaugy's spiritual connection to the life and influence of Jesus Christ. Although not a Christian, I was nevertheless deeply moved by the bold colors and powerful imagery. This artistic rendering affected me in a way that reading or hearing about Christian theology never could.

Artistic forms of expression extend the boundaries of how we come to know, by honoring multiple intelligences and indigenous knowledge. Artistic expression broadens cultural perspectives by allowing and honoring diverse ways of knowing and learning. Making space for creative expression in the adult education classroom and other learning communities helps learners uncover hidden knowledge that cannot easily be expressed in words. It opens up opportunities for adult learners to explore phenomena holistically, naturally, and creatively, thus deepening understanding of self and the world.

The term *art* as used throughout this chapter refers to all forms of artistic expression: poetry, drama, dance, literature, music, and all forms of visual art. The chapter considers both the aesthetics of art created by others and art created by students as part of the learning experience.

New Directions for Adult and Continuing Education, no. 107, Fall 2005 © Wiley Periodicals, Inc.

Limitations of Traditional Ways of Constructing Knowledge in Adult and Higher Education

Cognitive knowing has dominated the adult education classroom, where the curriculum typically emphasizes transmission of knowledge through cultural reproduction (Greene, 1995). We prize reading, writing, and intellectual discourse. The intent of this chapter is not to suggest that these forms of teaching and learning are inherently wrong; they draw on only part of our human potential. Expression through spoken or written language can be a limitation (Lawrence and Mealman, 2001). When we open up intellectual space to incorporate other ways of knowing into our teaching practice, as expressed through metaphor, dance, poetry, visual art, or dramatic expression, we draw on the affective, somatic, and spiritual domains. Participants can more fully express what they know. Barone and Eisner (1997), pioneers in the area of arts-based research, agree that rationalist modes of inquiry have served to suppress artistic modes of expression. If we insist that people put their ideas into words, what gets communicated is often partial or not expressed at all (Lawrence and Mealman, 2001).

Many educators, particularly those in formal education settings, are reluctant to encourage artistic forms of expression in their classrooms because they are themselves unfamiliar, and thus uncomfortable, with the affective dimensions of knowledge production. The question of evaluation often comes up. How does one assess learning from a painting or musical composition? I have found that engaging students as partners in the evaluation process is an essential component in evaluating nonrational work.

As a final integrative project at the completion of her master's program in adult education, one of my students created a quilt. Though it was beautifully crafted, viewing the quilt alone did not give me enough insight into the student's learning process. But as we sat together and she explained how the panels, colors, and symbols represented the building blocks of her learning, I was able to more clearly see and assess her learning. Spoken language is not always necessary to understand art (indeed, it seems almost paradoxical), but discussion can sometimes assist educators in the evaluation process, enabling their students to make use of these creative forms of expressing knowledge.

London (1989) believes that human intelligence lies above and below the conscious level. To know, we need to value and acknowledge the unknown. Adopting this unknowing state of mind opens us up to more creative possibilities; "a state of Not Knowing allows us greater facility in rearranging what we know into new configurations and definitions of reality" (p. 81). Artistic expression is a way of tapping into this unknown region.

Art as Indigenous Knowledge

We often hear it expressed that art is a universal language. One need not understand Japanese to appreciate the delicate brush strokes of Japanese watercolor. The bold colors of Diego Rivera speak to us whether our native language is Spanish, English, or Swahili. CD stores in the United States now have a category called world music, which includes native music from a variety of countries. Every culture and every tradition from earliest civilization to the present has created art, music, theater, poetry, and dance.

Eisner (1972) offered an "essentialist justification" (p. 2) for teaching art in schools. Although recognizing that art education serves to meet the needs of students and society, Eisner asserts that art is also indigenous unto itself. Art makes contributions to human society that are unique and cannot be duplicated by any other means. Art can also be a means to overcome the literacy barrier. McNeal (1997), who worked with an Inuit population in Western Canada, used films and tapes of cultural elders depicting indigenous history and culture to help reach her adult literacy students.

Our earliest ways of knowing are preverbal (Allen, 1995). Children naturally and spontaneously express themselves through singing, dancing, drawing, or acting out (pretending), often before they learn to read and write and sometimes even before they acquire a spoken language. At some point, this natural ability is thwarted. It may happen as we go to school and are told by the teacher that trees can't be blue, or that we must color inside the lines. We are told that our acting out is causing a disturbance. We are told that our singing voice is not in tune, so we stop singing. Our natural inclination can also be stifled by gender roles and expectations. When I was in the fourth grade and we had the opportunity to study a musical instrument in school, I was told that the saxophone was a "boy's instrument" and was encouraged to play the flute or violin. I did not join band that year, or ever. Is it any wonder then that by the time learners reach adulthood they are often reluctant to participate in artistic types of activity? As London (1989) expresses it, we have turned away from our natural ability to create as we learned to become embarrassed: "We have learned to feel so inept and disenfranchised from our own visual expressions that we simply cease doing it altogether" (p. xiii). Yet, as the chapters in this volume show, artistic expression is often the very medium that enables adult learning to occur.

Learning from Diverse Cultural Perspectives Through Art

As we recognize and appreciate that art is indigenous to all cultures, we can view it as a means to learn about diverse cultures and cultural perspectives. This understanding can assist us in helping our diverse learners get to know one another (see Lems in Chapter Two of this volume). We can also use the arts as a way to promote understanding of cultural perspectives that are not present within the learning group. We are all constrained by our positionality to a certain extent. We view the world through our race, gender, class, and ethnic identities.

Greene (1995) used the literature of African American and other women to present multiple realities, thus allowing learners to see the world through many lenses. Rather than relying on the history books to teach about slavery, she used fictional literature such as Toni Morrison's *Beloved* to allow her learners to consider history from the perspective of other's experiences. Similarly, Eisner (1995) stated that "artistically crafted work also has the capacity to put us in the shoes of those we do not know" (p. 2). This level of understanding can create a sense of empathy, which opens us up to even greater learning. As we come to know and care about individuals, we are more open to learning from and about them. Allen (1995) believes that images provide a means to communicate on a deeper level than words. These images can help us more readily transcend cultural boundaries.

Clover (2000), who studied community arts in the context of adult environmental education, found that art could be a way of overcoming socioeconomic as well as cultural barriers, as people who did not ordinarily move in the same circles came together to work on projects.

Opening ourselves to the potential of learning through cultural difference requires that we honor and respect diverse ways of learning, knowing, and expressing that knowledge. If we truly value our students and honor the fullness of who they are culturally and individually, we need to create opportunities for multiple modes of expression. If we accept only written or linguistic forms of expression and try to convert our students to these ways of knowing, we devalue who they are or who they may become (Lawrence and Mealman, 2001). By insisting that people speak our language rather than finding a common mode of communication such as through art, we do violence to them.

Knowing Self Through Art

Allen (1995) says that *art is a way of knowing*. We can come to know love, fear, work, patterns, and transformation through art. Most important, we can come to know ourselves. For Allen, this knowing comes from the creation of visual images through painting, drawing, or sculpture. The images come to us from our physical surroundings, our memories of past experience, our imagination, and our dreams. According to Dirkx (2001), it is important to pay attention to the emotional aspects of our learning process. Awareness of our emotional state comes to us in the form of images. These images help us connect our inner self with the outer world, which is what Dirkx refers to as "soul work" (2001, p. 69). Images can be expressed through various forms of art. Creation of art helps us make sense of self and the world in which we live.

In my adult learning classes, I sometimes ask the students (mean age forty) to draw images of themselves at different decades of their lives. The images and symbols that emerge are often indicative of their particular life tasks and help them understand their developmental processes. This level of self-knowledge is not limited to visual art. Knowing occurs through writing music, poetry, or prose, or through dance and theatrical expression. This knowledge can also occur through experiencing art created by others, as in listening to music, looking at photographs, or watching a play, particularly in the context of a class or adult learning group. The group can discuss the work from multiple perspectives and interpretations, thus taking advantage of the collaborative synergy and social construction of knowledge (Lawrence, 1996).

Eisner (1995) believes that experiencing art created by others can "create a paradox of revealing what is universal by examining what is particular" (p. 3). As we encounter fictional characters in literature or drama, we often recognize ourselves and others. A good example is the film *Educating Rita,* which has often been used with groups of returning adult learners. Women and men of all races and cultures typically identify with Rita, a young English beautician who decides to take classes at the Open University.

McNeal (1997) and her colleagues (white Canadians) found that including art in the curriculum was helpful in teaching across borders when they accepted an assignment north of the Arctic Circle with Inuit college students. They discovered that art was a way to connect people to their own history and culture. The arts program not only assisted the students in developing knowledge of self and culture; the teachers were enlightened as well.

Accessing or Uncovering Hidden Knowledge

The first time I bring crayons, colored markers, and sheets of newsprint into my graduate adult education classes, the students look at me in disbelief ("You want me to do what?" "Is this graduate school or kindergarten?"). Once they overcome their initial hesitancy and begin to draw, they are surprised to discover that they have tapped into a source of knowledge that was always present but veiled or hidden. Artistic expression allowed them to access this knowledge in ways that writing did not. Art draws on a source of wisdom within each of us that does not exist anywhere else (London, 1989). London believes that creating art can also be a means to uncover or reveal our original primal self: "There is an immediate sense of recognition, often accompanied by sorrow, later to be followed by quiet, but deep joy" (p. 44).

Greene (1995) argues in favor of including all forms of art in the school curriculum because of their great power to "release the imagination" (p. 27), which allows us to see the unseen. Art not only engages us at an intellectual level; it evokes feelings, intuitions, and even bodily sensations. Paying attention to these modes of experiencing can result in deeper knowledge.

Certain works of art, particularly those of the surrealists (notably René Magritte and Marcel Duchamp), recontextualize the familiar (Eisner, 1995). They force us to view familiar objects in new ways. In this sense we are not passive consumers of art; we are co-creators of an interpretive process. Art engages all of our senses, awakening our imaginative and intellectual capabilities.

Image Making as a Way to Deepen Understanding

As this chapter has attempted to point out, experiencing art that was created by others helps us see anew. Creating our own art calls on more of our own abilities to make sense of the world holistically. Willis (2002) exemplified both processes in his phenomenological study of adult education in aboriginal Australia. He used poetic expression to make sense of his data, thus gaining more insight into the experience of the phenomena. By creating a gallery of panels displaying his poetry, he made it possible for others to experience his research findings in a way that engaged them as co-interpreters in a meaning-making process.

Greene (1995) believes that art has a critical role in this process of meaning making: "It is difficult for me to teach educational history or philosophy to teachers-to-be without engaging them in the domain of imagination and metaphor. How else are they to make meaning out of the discrepant things they learn? How else are they to see themselves as practitioners, working to choose, working to teach in an often indecipherable world?" (p. 99)

Allen (1995) found that creating artistic images was a way to come to a deeper understanding of many of life's challenges, among them grief, fear, and the unknown. London (1989) believes that when we look at art or experience it we see it directly, firsthand, with "original eyes." This is especially true when we listen to a song or look at a photograph or painting of a significant event, as in my experience at the Awakenings Museum. We come to a deeper understanding than if we read about the event or hear about it from another source: "Seeing the thing directly is having an experience with all the complexity of thoughts and feelings and somatic reactions that accompany all experiences" (London, 1989, p. 53).

Learning Through the Arts

The arts are an ideal complement to the rational discourse that dominates most of academe. Although many academicians recognize the value of a fine arts curriculum in itself, there is little written that addresses using artistic expression in mainstream adult and higher education. I surmise that the paucity of literature is because we are not incorporating the arts into our practice to any great degree.

As previously stated, there is often a great deal of discomfort when adults are asked to draw, paint, or present a dramatic skit. My students often feel the need to preface sharing of their artwork by telling the group, "I'm not an artist"—those are the ones who are brave enough to attempt the activity at all. I suspect many educators also feel this discomfort. They avoid artistic expression because it raises the specter of learned childhood responses to being judged and evaluated by the quality of their art. It is much safer to stick to known pedagogical processes. As London (1989) suggests, we need to rid ourselves of these judgments about what is good and bad art in order to free our creative abilities. It is the process of creating art, not the product, that is most important. The process is where the learning takes place. Clover (2000) found this process element to be especially true in using art with adults working on community projects. The learning was in the collective process of creating, planning, and reflecting.

Cassou and Cubley (1995) teach painting as a spontaneous process without thought to the product or outcome. They pose questions such as: "What would I do if I painted something that didn't have to make sense?" (p. 100) and "What would I paint if no one were going to see it?" (p. 34) They make it safe it for their learners by encouraging them to let go of the inner critic and focus on the process. Letting go of this self-judgment or fear of judgment by others is an important first step for people engaging in artistic work. Once we allow the creativity to flow through us, we become agents in our own learning process (Greene, 1995). Learning becomes an active process rather than a passive one.

Art in the Curriculum

Eisner (1972), a pioneer in the field of arts-based education, informs us that knowing how people learn in art helps us know how to teach them. I would take that one step further. To create educational experiences through art, one must value art for its learning potential. Greene (1995) believes that incorporating arts into the curriculum leads to a "deepening and expanding mode of tuning in" (p. 104).

The chapters in this volume exemplify many ways in which educators of adults have incorporated various art forms into their teaching practice. A single art form can significantly enhance the curriculum, but a combination of arts can have dramatic results. Mullen (1999) and her colleagues developed an arts-based educational program for incarcerated women that blended visual art, movement, and writing into a health-and-wellness course. Collaboration among the inmates was facilitated as women wrote or created a visual expression of their experience. They created performances based on one another's writing. They wrote about each other's artwork. Outcomes of the program included personal and cultural awareness as well as communal expression.

Art forms used in combination also allow individual preferences and creativity to emerge. In a class on life history, I played flute music by Douglas Spotted Eagle, inviting students to reflect on significant life transition through visual art, writing, or movement. Some wrote poetry or prose, some drew pictures; one person created a collage, and another got up and performed a dance.

Art as a Means for Social Change

The arts, though not necessarily represented in mainstream literature, have frequently been a part of adult education in the context of social change. The most noted examples are popular theater, or "theater of the oppressed," which was developed by Augusto Boal (1995) in the tradition of Paulo Freire to empower people to solve their own problems. Two excellent examples of theater as a means for social change can be found in this volume. Donoho (Chapter Seven) describes an urban community performance project in the city of Chicago, while Noble (Chapter Five) discusses his work in theater with the mentally ill in western Canada.

Kamler (2001) combined theatrical performance with writing and video production in her work with women over the age of seventy. They wrote and performed stories of aging to educate the community beyond the cultural stereotypes typically held about the elderly.

Clover (2000) believes that art can be a means to increase community awareness of environmental issues, thus creating a catalyst for change. She describes a case study where artists, environmentalists, and sanitation workers came together to deal with the problem of waste management in the city of Toronto. They painted images on garbage trucks to raise community awareness about the problem. One benefit to the project was that disparate groups of people who lived in the same community but did not talk with one another came together to work on a common goal. Art was the universal language that allowed them to communicate, overcoming stereotypes to work for a common cause.

Implications for Adult Education

Incorporating various art forms—poetry, drama, music, literature, visual art, and others—into the practice of adult education provides tremendous potential to enhance both teaching and learning. For these learning opportunities to occur, educators need to take risks by venturing out of their comfort zone and in turn encouraging their students to take similar risks. The payoff for such risk taking is that more of our human potential is activated as we continue to learn how to learn.

References

Allen, P. B. *Art Is a Way of Knowing.* Boston: Shambhala, 1995.

Barone, T. E., and Eisner, E. "Arts-Based Educational Research." In R. M. Jaeger (ed.), *Complementary Methods for Research in Education.* Washington, D.C.: American Educational Research Association, 1997.

Boal, A. *The Rainbow of Desire: The Boal Method of Theatre and Therapy.* New York: Routledge, 1995.

Cassou, M., and Cubley, S. *Life, Paint and Passion.* New York: Tarcher/Putnam, 1995.

Clover, D. E. "Community Arts as Environmental Education and Activism: A Labour and Environment Case Study." *Convergence,* 2000, 33(4), 19–30.

Dirkx, J. M. "The Power of Feelings: Emotion, Imagination, and the Construction of Meaning in Adult Learning." In S. B. Merriam (ed.), *The New Update on Adult Learning Theory*. San Francisco: Jossey-Bass, 2001.

Eisner, E. *Educating Artistic Vision*. New York: Macmillan, 1972.

Eisner, E. W. "What Artistically Crafted Research Can Help Us Understand about Schools." *Educational Theory*, 1995, *45*(1), 1–6.

Greene, M. *Releasing the Imagination*. San Francisco: Jossey-Bass, 1995.

Kamler, B. "We're Not Nice Little Old Ladies." *Journal of Adolescent and Adult Literacy*, 2001, *45*(3), 232–35.

Lawrence, R. L. "Co-Learning Communities: A Hermeneutic Account of Adult Learning in Higher Education Through the Lived World of Cohorts." Dissertation, Northern Illinois University, 1996.

Lawrence, R. L., and Mealman, C. A. "The Researcher as Artist: Creating Pathways for Acquisition and Expression of Knowledge." Paper presented at the twentieth annual Midwest Research-to-Practice Conference in Adult, Continuing, and Community Education, Charleston, Illinois, Oct. 2001.

London, P. *No More Secondhand Art: Awakening the Artist Within*. Boston: Shambhala, 1989.

McNeal, J. "DBAE in an Arctic Fine Arts Program for Indigenous Canadian College Students." *Visual Arts Research*, 1997, *23*(2), 71–82.

Mullen, C. A. "Reaching Inside Out: Arts-Based Educational Programming for Incarcerated Women." *Studies in Art Education*, 1999, *40*(2), 143–161.

Willis, P. "Risky Journeys: Using Expressive Research to Portray Cross-Cultural Adult Educational Practice in Aboriginal Australia." (CD-ROM.) *Alberta Journal of Educational Research*, 2002, *48*(3).

Randee Lipson Lawrence is an associate professor in the department of Adult, Continuing, and Literacy Education at National-Louis University.

2

The unique magic of music in the English language learning classroom is explored, with emphasis on research, learning objectives, and rewards that come from using music regularly.

Music Works: Music for Adult English Language Learners

Kristin Lems

In twenty years of teaching adult English language learners (ELLs) in a number of instructional settings and at various levels, I have found one truth that continues to reverberate resoundingly across time and space: music works. Almost without exception, music-centered classroom activities in which I have engaged have yielded untold treasures—for the whole class, the individual students, and the instructor.

As I ponder all of the ways in which music has enlivened and animated my classrooms over the years, I keep coming back to the same simple observation: I like to be around people when they are experiencing music. They have a certain transfigured sweetness as they listen to music, as they sing. I've watched a tough Ukrainian mechanic with dirty fingernails transformed into a compelling, soulful singer before his astonished classmates. I've seen a shy young Chinese woman, covering her mouth as she laughed, finally stand and sing a Chinese folk song with spirit. I have witnessed the intensity when a Mexican student introduced the class to Selena's music and then cried as she reexperienced Selena's untimely death. I've watched a disaffected Polish punk rocker, complete with hair spikes, bring in a large collection of heavy-metal CDs and reveal that he knew much more English than he had ever let on.

This chapter is composed of three parts: a summary of research findings on music and second language learning; a set of learning objectives that can be addressed using music, with a description of sample activities that could serve each of the objectives; and some personal reflections about music in my own classrooms, along with a few rhetorical questions about the relative paucity of music activities in programs for adult ELLs.

New Directions for Adult and Continuing Education, no. 107, Fall 2005 © Wiley Periodicals, Inc.

The Research: Scarce, But Promising

There has been limited experimental research on music and second language learning, and even less with a focus on adults. This is changing, however, as new measurement tools become available, such as the PET (Positron Emission Tomography) scan, which shows the locations of brain activity (Sabbatini, 2004). At the same time, quite a few publications describe successful classroom activities using music. Sampling a bit from both, I cite some research involving music and second language learners, and then I summarize the accounts of successful classroom activities using music with ELL adults.

Recent developments in brain-based research note that central features of music and language are housed near one another in the human brain, suggesting they may share features of a "grammar" that orders musical elements and language elements similarly (Maess, Koelsch, Gunter, and Friederici, 2001). Music and language, both rule-based systems, "consist of discrete elements combined in hierarchical sequences—to serve as foils for each other" (Benson, 2003, p. 33), as one cognitive scientist described it.

Research supports a music-language connection with regard to learning a second language (Lems 2001, 2002). Lowe (1998) found that students in a French immersion program in Canada who learned music concepts and patterns daily along with their language study did significantly better in both foreign language study and music study than their peers who did not study music. Medina (1993) found that second grade ELLs who were taught vocabulary using supplementary music and pictures learned more words than those in groups using one, or neither, of the artistic enhancements, and Shunk (1999) found that ELLs learned the most new words when music and sign language supplemented their vocabulary lessons.

Murphey (1992), who has used music extensively with adult ELLs, theorized that lyrics in pop songs are especially effective in boosting language production because they contain high-frequency vocabulary—the words every learner needs to know—along with very few referents to place, time, pronoun, and gender. This creates an open-ended situation, allowing many kinds of background knowledge to come into play. In addition, songs tend to contain universal themes that make them easy for people to identify with, while creating an opportunity for "involuntary rehearsal" (Parr and Krashen, 1986, p. 275) of the new language within the brain.

Whether didactic value is inherent to the properties of songs or not, there is a resounding consensus that using them motivates and inspires adult learners. Green (1993) surveyed Puerto Rican college-level ESL students to see which among seventeen activities they considered enjoyable and which they considered helpful (effective). Listening to a song ranked number one for enjoyableness, and singing a song ranked fifth. The two musical activities were also ranked in the upper 50 percent of activities for effectiveness. Interestingly, the highest correlation between enjoyableness and effectiveness of all the activities was for singing an English-language song ($r = .760$ at $p < .05$). One student commented in the survey that listening to a song "is a complete learning in English" (1993, p. 6).

When Oxman (1975) used music in a special pullout program for at-risk high-school-aged ELLs, she noted a greater interest in school activities for the students using the music curriculum. Puhl (1989) found that using instrumental music for ELL activities with South African miners resulted in more vitality among the adults in the experimental group. In fact, numerous articles I have read make the same claim: students enjoy music, they open up to it, and they feel more relaxed in its presence. Quite simply, no better activity can be found as an overall in-class motivator. Put more colloquially, music rocks!

Learning Objectives and Music-Based Activities

Although many discrete learning goals can be served by musical activities, music's power should not simply be reduced to individual parts. Clearly, the whole is greater than the sum of the parts. As with other discussions of the arts and their "use" to society, one arrives at a point where the value of an artistic experience cannot be easily measured in numbers or words. This very power to move beyond words and numbers makes the arts vulnerable to being underfunded, unfunded, or unacknowledged in the curriculum. Because the arts inhabit a different realm, and because music is, finally, music, courses that feature it are few and far between, in both the K–12 classroom and adult education. Even using written words to describe music can result in a "poor translation," but words are what we have to express what is so often beyond words. How I wish this chapter had a mechanism to allow music to play softly as you read it, so the music could speak for itself!

Positive Attitude and Affect

It is widely understood that what adults bring to the classroom is at least as important as what the classroom offers them. An adult listening to music has a rich frame of reference constructed from his or her own lived experiences, no less rich if the adult has been out of school a long time or hasn't gone far in formal education. Moreover, no culture has an "inferior" music. All of the forms of music around the world suit their culture to a T, because the cultures create and adapt them constantly.

An immigrant adult transplanted to a new cultural and linguistic environment has many funds of knowledge (Moll, 1992) to draw on but may not be able to express them, because of the language barrier. Enjoyment of music, however, has universal appeal and creates a welcoming embrace for all, including those who can't yet find the words. Anyone can enjoy a melody, whether by listening, humming, whistling or singing to it, or even by dancing along. Music, in its joyful din, welcomes all learners in and gets toes tapping, hands clapping, heads nodding, and faces smiling. It is in plentiful supply for minimal cost and can relax a whole roomful of people in a minute. Who could ask for more?

For creating classroom atmosphere, many teachers swear by classical instrumental music, though many kinds of music can create a positive "soundtrack" for students' lives. To relax my adult Polish immigrants, for example, I sometimes bring CDs of Chopin's piano music and play it in the background. Whether or not they have any training in classical music, whether they are laborers or former doctors, Chopin's music draws a universally positive response not only because of its beauty but because it tells them that I know and honor the music of one of their great artists. In turn, they discover that something they cherish from their homeland is still available to them and is acknowledged as important by others. At the same time, students from other backgrounds in the class are given an opportunity to experience and relish an aspect of their classmates' Polish heritage, which builds a climate of collaboration and trust.

Listening Comprehension

Listening to songs is a tried-and-true method by which students can improve their listening comprehension in a new language, and when used as a guided activity its value is maximized even further. Improving listening comprehension is probably the primary use of music in the ELL classroom; there are innumerable ways to organize the activity to ensure success.

One lesson usable with any age is to choose a song, create several copies of its lyrics in large type, laminate them, cut the lyrics into lines, put students in small groups, and have them arrange the lines in the correct order as they listen to the song. To optimize the benefits of the listening, the song lyrics should be just slightly above the students' current proficiency level, though not too far (Vygotsky, 1978). The activity can also be performed as a race among several groups, to see which one can put the lyrics in order first. If long tables are not available for laying out the lyrics, they can be placed on the floor in various corners of the room, with students clustered around them on hands and knees.

Usually, playing the song twice is enough time to put the lines in order, but a more challenging song might have to be played four or five times. Judicious use of the Pause button can reduce the number of times the song is heard. A variation is to see how many lines can be put in order even before hearing the song, on the basis of its structure or narrative line. Then the listening becomes confirmatory and reinforces a hypothesis that the students themselves make.

Picking songs is an art in itself, and many articles have been devoted to this topic. Talking about criteria and caveats for choosing songs could swamp the remainder of this chapter and still not exhaust the subject. After all is said and done, I would simply advise that the instructor pick songs he or she really likes, because when a teacher likes a song the lesson plan is almost always clever and thoughtful, and the enthusiasm the song generates in the teacher carries over to the students.

Oral and Pronunciation Practice

For adult students who are already literate in their first language, reading English can result in confusion because of the mismatch between the sounds they expect from the alphabet letters and the sounds they actually hear. Reading along with a song is a great way to close that gap and at the same time improve pronunciation. For example, students can be asked to circle all of the occurrences of the American "flap" sound as they listen to a song (the flap is the distinctive *t* sound in American English that occurs between two vowels or a vowel and an *r*, such as the words "city" or "party"). This unusual feature of American English throws students off when they first come to the United States or study with an American teacher, and the sound needs to be explained and practiced. Songs are the perfect medium to do so.

Song lyrics can easily be chanted or sung, aiding oral fluency and pronunciation. At the same time, the rhythmic contour of a song usually (but not always) matches the natural stress patterns of spoken English and aids students in developing their oral expressiveness through natural practice.

In addition to examining parts of a song, songs can be learned from beginning to end. Since I enjoy singing in class, I often give students a stapled packet of song lyrics at the beginning of the quarter (in accordance with fair-use policy for song lyrics) and teach them to sing a new song from it every week. By the end of the quarter, the students can sing ten new songs without assistance. Sometimes they even memorize them. Even more impressively, they remember these songs long after the course is over—and sing me the melodies when they come back to visit years later.

Songsheets should include complete written credits for every song and should indicate how students can buy a recording of each one. These days, this is an easy task, with Internet options available for crediting and purchasing most recorded music.

Teachers sometimes ask how I "get" my students to sing. Often, the issue is not only that students won't sing but that some teachers feel uncomfortable doing so. I'd urge any such teacher to rethink the fear. Instead of conceptualizing the classroom singing as a "performance," it can be reframed as a sort of "indoor campfire circle" (we know that everyone sings at one of those!). If you must, turn the lights down and crack out the marshmallows . . . whatever it takes.

In many years of teaching songs to adult learners, I can count on the fingers of one hand students who would not take part in the singing. Besides, even if a student isn't singing, it doesn't mean he or she isn't listening, or learning, or enjoying the song. It just means the student isn't singing. People from most cultures of the world are far more comfortable singing aloud than are Americans today (although karaoke and TV star searches are changing that somewhat). This being the case, teachers of immigrant and foreign students can learn from their students and increase their own enjoyment with music. Teachers can indeed heal themselves.

For those irrevocably opposed to singing alone, I would suggest buying a set of sing-along tapes or karaoke CDs. Reasonably priced tapes with lyrics booklets and notated melodies with chords can be found in a bookstore or even a toy store; they cover many themes, including a lot of "Americana" of interest to new immigrants. Karaoke requires a special machine, but more and more people own them, and they are increasingly affordable for purchase by educational programs as well. The scrolling words and full musical arrangements of karaoke make students feel comfortable as they sing.

Writing Activities

Music is a natural stimulus for giving students a chance to free-write, or even free-draw, as they listen. Drawing or writing to exciting and dramatic instrumental music, such as Tchaikovsky, Moussorgsky, or other nineteenth-century composers, can be followed by sharing the writing or showing the drawings to the class. If the class follows a more grammar-based curriculum, students can do structured writing at the paragraph or sentence level, or if they are at a beginner level follow a fill-in-the-blank template.

For example, I teach my high-beginner-level students the song "El Condor Pasa," a lyrical poem by Paul Simon set to an Andean flute melody by Daniel Robles. It has very evocative language, beginning with "I'd rather be a sparrow than a snail" (Simon, Milchburg, and Robles, 2003). After we talk about all the lyrics, I ask them to write their own sentences using the structures: "I'd rather be _____ than _____" and "I'd rather _____ than _____."

The first sentence supplies the verb and only requires two parallel nouns or adjectives in the blanks. The second sentence requires adding a verb along with the nouns or adjectives. From this seemingly limited, restrictive activity, I have received such poetic sentences as these:

"I'd rather be water than a fire."
"I'd rather be an unknown person than famous."
"I'd rather stay in childhood than grow up."

Clearly, even sentence-level writing can be quite expressive, and modeling sentences on song lyrics can, like poetry, bypass small talk and get to deep thoughts and feelings straightaway.

Another fruitful assignment is to ask students to write a composition on a musical topic. Sometimes I ask them to write a composition about their favorite piece of music. I ask them to give a little background, explain why it is special to them, and then bring a recording of the piece of music to class to share. They read the composition they wrote about the piece or the artist to the class and then play the piece.

It is also possible to use a music topic in a computer-assisted assignment, such as comparing biographies of a favorite rap star at two or more fan sites and arranging the information from them into a Venn diagram. Then the students can use higher-order thinking to critically evaluate the information in the two sites (leading to strategies such as questioning the author or writing for a purpose).

Reading Comprehension, Vocabulary Building, and Culture

There are few texts better than song lyrics for capturing a student's interest. The enormous popularity of lyrics Web sites is testament to this. Once lyrics are available, however they are introduced, their words and phrases can be probed and put to use. Like poetry, lyrics can be examined on (at least) two levels: the structure, and the literary theme. What's more, when you share lyrics with immigrant students a third dimension is added: cultural themes. American songs are a rich source of contemporary idioms and culture, and in fact many concepts and traditions have entered American culture through the medium of song. Consider some representative examples of the pervasive influence songs have on the culture:

- It was through song lyrics that Americans got the widespread tradition of tying a yellow ribbon around a tree to remember someone (from the song "Tie a Yellow Ribbon"; Levine and Brown, 1973). Today, yellow ribbons, lately in the form of magnetized bumper stickers, are used to convey support for U.S. troops stationed overseas.
- Song lyrics introduced the concept of cheerful determinism to listeners around the world in "Que Sera, Sera" (sung by Doris Day; Livingston and Evans, 2000[1955]).
- We learn that we can demand not just generic respect but "R-E-S-P-E-C-T," spelled out in full, when we want to be sure we get it (from the song "Respect," sung by Aretha Franklin; Redding, 1965).
- Songs introduce colorful and memorable characters not originally found in written text, as with Rudolph the Red-Nosed Reindeer and Frosty the Snowman (in songs by the same names).

Introducing songs with useful phrases and concepts enables adult ELLs to have access to those concepts and helps them accommodate to their new environment. Also, listening to songs is a good way for immigrants and foreign students to access the pronunciation and slang terms found in dialect groups and subcultures, especially the language of Black English, which is strongly represented in all genres of pop music. Finally, being familiar with a number of songs gives students a ready topic of conversation with native speakers, which, like "the weather," is pleasant, open-ended, and safe.

Music is able to take ELLs in two directions at once: it can allow them to interact with the new culture in which they are living, and at the same time it gives an opportunity to bring the music of their homeland to others. When students have an opportunity to bring music from their homeland into the classroom, it affirms their cultural roots, creates a venue for making new friends, and fosters continuity between old and new experiences.

Songs can be played during a class party or a break, even if they don't have a single word of English in them. In some of my classes, I set up a schedule in which each student has a chance to bring a favorite CD to be played during a break. This has led to many animated exchanges as students seek information about musicians they like from cultures other than their own.

Last year, a student brought a CD by the British group Cold Play. I was dubious that it was a real band because I had never heard of it (my, what teacher arrogance!). Sure enough, they won a major 2003 Grammy award, and a huge billboard on a busy Chicago street now advertises that a certain radio station airs a lot of Cold Play. Just think: I am a little bit less uncool thanks to my immigrant students!

A Call for More Music

Browsing through the table of contents of an ESL reader reveals that music is a common reading topic. Apparently, publishers have found that students really enjoy music topics, and such articles abound. Yet there is only one published song-based curriculum for adults, called "Sing It!" and compiled by Millie Grenough (1994); it is no longer in print. A glance at the program book for any professional ESL convention reveals many workshops in using music to teach ESL; in my personal experience as a presenter and attendee, such workshops tend to attract an overflow crowd. Still, there appears to be little institutional support for putting music in a prominent place in any ESL program. In fact, aside from my own workshops, I am aware of only one music-based ESL course at an American University, "English Through Music," an elective taught by Lorene Cleary at the University of California-Santa Barbara Extension ("English Through Music," 2003). Similarly, only one journal is devoted to the arts and language learning, the wonderful *Journal of the Imagination in Language Learning*.

Somehow, despite its power to enthrall and inspire, music is not on the short list as a method or content-area topic in English language teaching curricula. Since there are no adult ESL programs that put music at the center, it's hard to come by research showing the power of music as a teaching tool. Thus the cycle continues: students love learning about and experiencing music, teachers know that music works, but no one is empowered to take the next step of putting it in the center of a curriculum; consequently there is no "proof" that music helps with English. It's time to break the cycle, trust the testimony of hundreds of teachers and learners, and offer some music-based adult ESL courses, carefully collecting information on the results not only for skills development but for the affective domain as well.

At the parties I always hold on the final day of class, music is part of the closure, the fond farewell, which leaves us all, quite literally, with a song in our hearts. I wouldn't have it any other way.

References

Benson, E. "Making Sense of Chords and Conversations: New Research Is Exploring How the Brain Processes Music and Language." *APA Monitor on Psychology*, 2003, *34*(7), 32–36.

"English Through Music." English courses, University of California, Santa Barbara Extension. Retrieved Nov. 1, 2003 (http://www.unex.ucsb.edu/ip/english/courses/#).

Green, J. M. "Student Attitudes Toward Communicative and Non-Communicative Activities: Do Enjoyment and Effectiveness Go Together? *Modern Language Journal*, 1993, *77*(1), 1–10.

Grenough, M. *Sing It!* New York: McGraw-Hill, 1994.

Lems, K. "Using Music in the Adult ESL Classroom." *ERIC Digests*. Washington, D.C.: Center for Applied Linguistics, ERIC Clearinghouse on Languages and Linguistics, 2001.

Lems, K. "Music Hath Charms for Literacy in the ESL Classroom." *Indiana Reading Journal*, 2002, *34*(3), 6–12.

Levine, I., and Brown, L. R. "Tie a Yellow Ribbon Round the Ole Oak Tree." (Song.) New York: Levine and Brown Music, 1973.

Livingston, J., and Evans, R. "Que Sera Sera." (Song.) Los Angeles: Jay Livingston Music, 2000. (Originally published ASCAP, 1955)

Lowe, A. S. "L'enseignement de la Musique et de la Langue Seconde: Pistes d'Integration et Consequences sur les Apprentissages." *Canadian Modern Language Review*, 1998, *54*(2) 218–238.

Maess, B., Koelsch, S., Gunter, T. C., and Friederici, A. D. "Musical Syntax Is Processed in Broca's Area: An MEG Study." *Nature Neuroscience*, 2001, *4*, 540–545.

Medina, S. L. "The Effect of Music on Second Language Vocabulary Acquisition." *National Network for Early Language Learning*, 1993, *6*(3). (Also available from ERIC Document Reproduction Service, no. ED 352834.)

Moll, L. C. "Funds of Knowledge for Teaching: Using a Qualitative Approach to Connect Homes and Classrooms." *Theory into Practice*, 1992, *31*(2), 132–141.

Murphey, T. "The Discourse of Pop Songs." *TESOL Quarterly*, 1992, *26*(4), 770–774.

Oxman, W. "Music Language Arts Program: Spring 1975." Brooklyn: New York City Board of Education, 1975. (ERIC Document Reproduction Service, ED138684.)

Parr, P. C., and Krashen, S. "Involuntary Rehearsal of Second Languages in Beginning and Advanced Performers." *System*, 1986, *14*, 275—278.

Puhl, C. A. "Up from Under: English Training on the Mines." Report on 1988 Research Project Conducted at Gold Fields Training Services. Stellenbosch, South Africa: University of Stellenbosch, 1989. (ERIC Document Reproduction Service ED335864.)

Redding, O. "Respect." (Song.) Memphis, Tenn.: Stax Records, 1965.

Sabbatini, R. M. E. "The PET Scan: A New Window into the Brain." Retrieved Aug. 11, 2004 (http://www.epub.org.br/cm/n01/pet/pet.htm).

Shunk, H. A. "The Effect of Singing Paired with Signing on Receptive Vocabulary Skills of Elementary ESL Students." *Journal of Music Therapy*, 1999, *36*(2), 110–124.

Simon, P., Milchburg, J., and Robles, D. "El Condor Pasa" ("If I could"). (Song.) *Simon and Garfunkel's Greatest Hits*. New York: CBS, 1972.

Vygotsky, L. *Mind in Society: The Development of Higher Psychological Process*. Cambridge, Mass.: Harvard University Press, 1978.

Kristin Lems is an associate professor at National-Louis University, where she teaches English as a Second Language and is also a professional folksinger and songwriter (www.kristinlems.com).

3

The potential of poetry for expanding possibilities in teaching, learning, and research is explored through specific examples from a poet/teacher's practice of poetry as a way of knowing and a medium for sharing knowledge.

Lessons from the Anhinga Trail: Poetry and Teaching

Anne McCrary Sullivan

The Anhinga Trail in May: A Note to the Visitor

This is the subtle season. Waters have risen,
waters have spread, hundreds of long-legged birds
have flown to nesting sites. Alligators cool
in the dense grasses, underwater, in mud.
(Watch for their eyes or a rough bit of armor.)
This is the season that summons your alertness,
your good keen eye. Pay attention. There are clues
in the grasses beside the trail—that patch of sandy
earth, broken eggs of the softshell turtle, nest
robbed by raccoons or crows. In every season,
there is drama here. The strangler fig is always murdering.
You arrive to the chants of pig frogs. Tune your ear
to those groans in deep vegetation.
Focus your eye on the expanse of sawgrass prairie,
see—a river with tree islands.
Look down at bubbles rising to the water's surface
(there's something down there).
Watch for the Florida gar, ancient fish
with armor under its skin.

"I Came to the Everglades with a Grief" and "Anhinga Pairing" appeared first in *The Southern Review*, Spring 2004. "The Anhinga Trail in May: A Note to the Visitor" has been published internally at Everglades National Park. Anne McCrary Sullivan is copyright holder for all three poems.

Look deep into the pond apple trees; let your eyes find
the nest of sticks, the furry bodies of green heron chicks.
Soon they will be chirping; you can follow your ear.
Near the nests, sprays of tiny orchids.
Your alertness will not fail you, and you will see
what many miss in this subtle season beyond the dry
season's obvious teeming. Later, when mosquito bites
have calmed (it is also their season), when you are home,
check the leafy branches of remembering.
See what has nested there.

This is the only poem I have ever written as a deliberate act of instruction,
or (to use the language of informal education) interpretation. In my usual
professional life, my students are K–12 teachers who are working on a master's degree. I bring poetry into that formal context in a number of ways, and
I will talk about some of them, but I'd like to talk first about this poem; how
I came to write it; and what it exemplifies about some of the potential relations of poetry, teaching, and learning.

Poetry in Informal Adult Education

During a yearlong sabbatical, I spent the month of January as poet-in-res-
idence at Everglades National Park. This was my first visit to the park, and
I was astonished at the rich and beautiful diversity into which I had come.
I arrived in the dry season, which is a season teeming with wildlife. As
waters decrease from evaporation and lack of rainfall, creatures dependent
on water gather at the remaining sloughs and water holes. Every day I
would go to the Anhinga Trail, which runs alongside and then loops over
Taylor Slough, where at any time of day alligators were abundant, often
sunning themselves in piles; where every variety of heron waded or
perched, and ibis and wood storks stirred the shallow waters with their
feet. Turtles bobbed and sunned and swam just beneath the surface. Cor-
morants lined the rails and anhinga dived, then stood on low branches
with their wings spread to dry. It was, clearly—anyone could see—an
extraordinary place.

I learned a lot during that month. The poems I wrote grew out of an
intense engagement with the place itself and the field guides and resources
I carried around in my backpack. In March, I went to spend another month
in the park. This time I went as an interpretive volunteer. My responsibilities included roving interpretation on the Anhinga Trail. In March, the
change of seasons was beginning. The numbers of birds had decreased.
There was a somewhat subdued level of activity in comparison with January's near frenzy. But there was plenty to point to, talk about, place in the
context of the ecosystem.

When I returned in May, the rains had come. I was in a place very different from the one I had known in January. Interpretation was more challenging and, for me, in a way more interesting. It was the challenge of teaching visitors how to see beneath the quiet surfaces, how to read the subtleties of the season. I observed that many of the thousands of visitors had no access to interpretation. Many arrived before and after the hours of the visitor center, or when there was no scheduled walk or talk, no roving interpreter on the trail. I had occasion to overhear on a number of occasions that there was "nothing here." This troubled me, led to the urge to write the poem—a deliberate attempt to offer some help in how to read this place at this time of year.

The head of the Division of Interpretation for the area had the poem posted in the bulletin case near the head of the trail. I have no way of knowing how many people actually read it as they pass by or pause. But I'm pretty sure that it gets read more often than an explanatory essay or article on the same topic would if it were posted there. One of the opportunities that a poem offers us as an educational tool is its compression. Poems get a lot of work done in a small space. The poet, using the skills that enable compression, packs a world into a tennis ball. The reader, through attentive reading, unpacks that world in a matter of moments.

Educators in some informal contexts usually have very little time in which to communicate something significant: the length of a trail walk, for example, or a museum, arboretum, or aquarium visit. In his classic *Interpreting Our Heritage* (1977 [1957]), Freeman Tilden articulates six principles of interpretation that have become guiding concepts for many park rangers and other informal educators who are tasked with teaching in a compressed time frame. In my work as an interpretive volunteer, I have sometimes incorporated one or more poems into my interactions with visitors to the Everglades because the poems seem to assist with the objectives of the first of Tilden's principles.

Principle one: "Any interpretation that does not somehow relate what is being displayed or described to something within the personality or experience of the visitor will be sterile" (p. 9). In other words, information alone is sterile. People need some sense of connection with what they are looking at, or it is meaningless. Usually, when I am leading a walk on the Anhinga Trail, I have with me several poems from which to choose if a "teachable moment" arises. For example, when anhingas are nesting within sight of the trail, I sometimes pull out of my pocket this poem:

Anhinga Pairing

When the male anhinga's bright blue eye ring comes,
when he displays his fine feathers, raising his tail,
waving the wings, she begins to pay attention.
Then they swoop and glide together

near the nesting area—preen together, lifting
and fluffing feathers, rubbing each other's bills.
But they are not a pair until he finds the perfect
twig, offers it to her and she accepts.
Last year we saw him offer a twig, and she took it.
Even as we were all saying "Ahhh . . ." she lifted
that stick and hit him in the head with it, flew away.
Acceptance means something. And when she does
accept, they become *monogamous in a bond that lasts*
several years. What I haven't been able to learn
is how they go about separation. Is it mutual, a sort of inherent
biological timing? Or does one just leave? And for the other,
is there grief?

Poetry as an Educational Strategy

The graduate program in which I teach is an unusual one in many ways, not
the least of which is that I have the privilege of working with K–12 teachers through the whole two years of their program, teaching multiple courses
of an integrated curriculum and guiding their action research projects. There
is often a great deal of anxiety among my students as they enter a program
structured differently from anything they've previously experienced. They
don't know what to expect. They want certainties. They especially want an
outline for their research, a pattern to follow, a set of predetermined steps
that ensure success. I offer them guidelines, principles, a variety of strategies for data collection, but no single approach to the final representation
of their research. Each of them is expected to determine the final form of
the research project on the basis of the nature of the project and the abilities and inclinations of the researcher. One strategy I use to help them
increase their tolerance for ambiguity capitalizes on the compressed nature
of the poem.

The Poem as Research

As I begin this activity, I do not tell them we are going to be poem making.
As we move through it, I ask for a degree of tolerance for ambiguity by not
telling them where we are going. Generally, they seem to be having fun and
do not protest or seem uncomfortable as we move through a sequence. First,
I distribute stacks of newspapers to their tables along with a pair of scissors
for each person. Then I instruct them, one step at a time:

1. Cut from these newspapers a collection of words or short phrases that
   you like or that seem to have some connection with your life. You have
   twenty minutes in which to make your collection. If you run out of
   newspaper, trade with someone else.

2. For the next ten minutes, collect only nouns.
3. For the next ten minutes, collect only verbs.
4. For the next five minutes, collect conjunctions and prepositions.
5. Clear away the newspapers.

Then I distribute manila file folders. I hold up a folder, open it vertically.

6. This is your page. On this page, selecting from the words and phrases you have collected, construct a poem. The subject of the poem is *you*.

In the initial stages of construction, there is generally talk and some nervousness at the tables, but at some point in the process the room becomes completely silent as they engage in the concentrated thinking required for composition, as they move words, positioning and repositioning on the page. I have observed this phenomenon over and over again. As they work, I distribute glue sticks, and when the composition is ready, when they have finished gluing it all down, we share our poems. Finally, I ask them the question that is almost always answered first by a general, puzzled silence: "What does this activity have to do with research?"

What Does This Activity Have to Do with Research?

After an initial silence, they begin to make tentative observations, and little by little they piece together an understanding of how the poem-making activity has been analogous to the action research in which they are engaging.

Newspapers represent the *field of research,* with its inherent limits and boundaries. They go into that field, engage in *data gathering,* collecting whatever catches their attention and interest, guided by the broad focus of the self. During the process of data gathering, they have no preconceived idea of what they will do with these fragments. When I ask them to construct a poem, they are at first dismayed, afraid they will be able to make nothing of this disparate collection, but as they begin to lay out the fragments and examine them, they begin to perceive relations. They begin to *construct meaning* and *generate form.* No one fails to do this.

After the fact, we recall what they have read in Caine and Caine's synthesis of brain research (1994) with implications for teaching and learning: the human brain is hard wired for perceiving patterns, making meaning. We can't *not* do it. Concluding the activity, I restate for them, reassure them, that they have just demonstrated they have all the necessary cognitive skills and propensities for successful completion of their action research projects, including determination of the final form of the project to be based on the nature of the data in front of them. Later, some students indicate that this activity was a turning point for them; a point from which they were able to trust themselves and the process, tolerating its ambiguities and the fact that I would not give them an explicit pattern for the final product.

In a poem, hours may be compressed into a line, monumental life experiences compressed onto a page; in our poetry-making activity the two-year research process (in schematic form) is compressed into an evening.

The Found Poem

Our newspaper poems are a particular genre of poetry known as *found poetry*. Found poems are, quite simply, poems constructed of language that is found and arranged, rather than of language one generates. There are many varieties of found poem and many educational uses for them.

The making of a found poem can offer a nonthreatening way for adults whose literacy is limited, or speakers of other languages, to gain access to poetic expression in English (Kazemek and Rigg, 1995). It is a strategy that gives people at all levels of literacy a tool for focusing, selecting, and interpreting a particular text (Gorrell, 1989) or set of data (Butler-Kisber, 2002). It offers a compressed way of sharing research results in any field of qualitative inquiry, and it is particularly useful as a way of interpreting and representing interviews, retaining the original language of the interviewees. Carol Burg (2004), for example, has crafted poems from the language of people whom she interviewed about quilts. Cynthia Cannon Poindexter (2002) constructs poems from interviews with an HIV-positive couple. The resultant poems become useful for teaching in the fields for which the poems are relevant.

In another approach, I have sometimes constructed poems from texts that students are required to read, as a way of arousing interest and giving them entry. This strategy has been particularly useful when the texts are difficult to read or conceptually challenging. The work of John Dewey, for example, often seems hard for my students. Over time, I have developed a sequence of found poems from several of his books (Sullivan, 2000a). These poems focus on key ideas and are most often shaped from sections of the text that include concrete language. They are a springboard for prereading discussion, a sort of orientation that has seemed helpful. Here is an example of a found poem, which I constructed, from Dewey's *School and Society* (1990 [1900, 1902]):

Criminal

For one child
to help another—
school crime.

On some occasions, I ask students themselves to construct found poems from their reading. The poems suggest a lot about how they have understood the text and what they have considered important. It becomes a mode of assessment.

The Poems We Read and the Poems We Make

Most often, when poetry is brought into the arena of teaching and learning it is in the role of mnemonic device—a sort of painless trick for remembering ("I before E, except after C"). This works. It is useful. It only begins, however, to scratch the surface of what poetry can contribute to significant processes for learning about ourselves, our world, and each other.

The poems we read can take us across boundaries, give us vicarious experience, render the abstract concrete, take us under the skin of the other, generate empathy. I have often brought poems from *Unsettling America: An Anthology of Contemporary Multicultural Poetry* (Gillan and Gillan, 1994) into my teaching. This is a book whose explicit project is to complicate "the nostalgic vision of a simple, harmonious past," to present poems that "directly address the instability of American identity and confront the prevalence of cultural conflict and exchange within the United States" (p. xix). These poems bring us into the voices and perspectives of Mexican Americans, Japanese Americans, Native Americans, a multitude of Americans, speaking directly from experience and heritage, offering us in compressed form a complex, alternative view of U.S. history, keeping that history close to its human pulse.

The poems we make can bring us into closer relation with our concerns and their inherent tensions. They can teach us—they demand of us—a particular kind of attention (Sullivan, 2000b). They are a strategy for knowing more deeply, and they offer us an alternative way of interpreting and representing what we see, hear, and know.

Let's go back to the Anhinga Trail. For the period of my sabbatical, that trail was the site of significant learning. I arrived with no prior knowledge of the ecosystem or its inhabitants. Shocked by the wonder of its teeming diversity, I wanted intensely to make poems that would adequately represent it. To do so, I had to have details—had to observe closely, study movements and behaviors. I read, asked questions, followed rangers around with tape recorders. Once my interest was aroused, the poem became both the strategy and the purpose for learning.

At the same time I was studying the world around me, I was learning my way through an internal conflict. As I worked to construct poems of the concrete, sensory world, I discovered metaphorical implications that touched my internal concerns. The poems themselves became profoundly a way of knowing the dynamics of my interior world as well as those of the Everglades. Sometimes they clarified my thinking and feeling; sometimes they surprised me.

I Came to the Everglades with a Grief

This is what I have learned: weeping for beauty
replaces weeping for grief. Stunned at first
by the blue heron's crest, the purple gallinule's

iridescence, grief now creeps as surely forward
as this subtle river of grass flows south.
It goes about its quiet work stealthy
as the yellow panther in the understory,
necessary, as everything here is necessary
each to the other in a complex ecology.
Yesterday, only once I felt it moving. It lifted
like a bird from the expanse of sawgrass,
startled me. I had stopped looking for it.
This grief is learning to ride the anhinga, glide
and flap through forgiving air. It lands in bark-stained
water, dives beneath the surface, swims—I see it there,
indistinct shape, a quivering blur. On the bank,
the gator's black back stretched in sun
amazes me, makes me think that I can touch
a fine living leather with claws and teeth.

Poetry's demand for compression forces one to focus on what matters. Its demand for concreteness (Sullivan, 2004) allows some of this focusing to happen at a subconscious level. Why am I drawn to particular concrete details of the observed world? Sometimes I don't know until after the poem is written. Then the poem teaches me about my own inner workings. In some cases, there is a sort of solace or relief in giving form to what is troubling. Form making allows a sense of control where there may in fact be little or no control over external realities. This is part of what people mean when they speak of the therapeutic value of making poems (Orr, 2002; Dewey 1980 [1934]). It is a far more complex matter than simple expression of emotion. These are important things to teach.

Poetry as a Way of Knowing

There is a growing body of literature addressing poetry (and other arts) as a way of knowing (Dewey, 1980 [1934]; Eisner, 1985; Richardson, 1993; Barone and Eisner, 1997; Sullivan, 2000b; Butler-Kisber, 2002; Feldman, 2004; Hussey, 2004; Burg, 2004). The idea itself is certainly not new. Gregory Orr (2002, p. 1) reminds us that "lyric poetry is written down or composed in every culture on the planet at this moment, which means something like one thousand different cultures and three thousand different languages." Poetry as a way of negotiating experience, of attending to external and internal worlds, of bringing diverse worlds into close relation for arriving at renewed perception, is indigenous. Our particular technocratic culture, however—with its tendency to fragment, its demands for statistical relevance and measurable knowledge—has grown alienated from poetry as a way of knowing and from poetry in general.

When poetry is taught in school, it is more often than not taught as a set of rules and procedures, with a terminology that relates to measurement of lines and stanzas, identification of elements and forms. Poems become riddles to which only the English teacher has the answer. As a result, very few of the teachers with whom I work report, coming into the program, a relationship with poetry. It becomes part of my task to lead them to that particular source of pleasure and insight; to poetry as a way of being in and knowing the world; a way of seeing what matters; a way of arriving at and sharing perception; a strategy for compressed holistic vision. But poetry is not just for teachers. Many of our best-known poets have lived the life of poetry from within a distinctly different profession. Wallace Stevens was an insurance executive. William Carlos Williams, a physician, often scribbled drafts of poems on a prescription pad between rounds. George Gopen (1984), a law professor and poet, has proposed that "poetry is the best preparation for the study of law" (p. 333). Because poetry is inherently a way of being in relation with the world, it is a strategy for us all. This is something our culture has forgotten. It is something I hope we will relearn.

References

Barone, T., and Eisner, E. "Arts-Based Educational Research." In R. Jaeger (ed.), *Complementary Methods for Research in Education* (2nd ed.). Washington, D.C.: American Educational Research Association, 1997.

Burg, C. "Ordinary Fabrics, Unseen Stories." *Journal of Critical Inquiry into Curriculum and Instruction,* 2004, 5(2), 15–20.

Butler-Kisber, L. "Artful Portrayals in Qualitative Inquiry: The Road to Found Poetry and Beyond." *Alberta Journal of Educational Research,* 2002, 48(3), 229–239.

Caine, R. N., and Caine, G. *Making Connections: Teaching and the Human Brain.* Reading, Mass.: Addison-Wesley, 1994.

Dewey, J. *Art as Experience.* New York: Perigee Books, 1980. (Originally published 1934)

Dewey, J. *The School and Society* and *The Child and The Curriculum* (expanded ed.). Chicago: Centennial Publications, University of Chicago, 1990. (Works originally published in 1900 and 1902)

Eisner, E. "Aesthetic Modes of Knowing." In E. Eisner (ed.), *Learning and Teaching the Ways of Knowing.* Chicago: University of Chicago Press, 1985.

Feldman, R. "Poetic Representation of Data in Qualitative Research." *Journal of Critical Inquiry into Curriculum and Instruction,* 2004, 5(2), 10–14.

Gillan, M. M., and Gillan, J. *Unsettling America: An Anthology of Contemporary Multicultural Poetry.* New York: Penguin, 1994.

Gopen, G. "Rhyme and Reason: Why the Study of Poetry Is the Best Preparation for the Study of Law." *College English,* 1984, 46(4), 333–347.

Gorrell, N. "Let Found Poetry Help Your Students Find Poetry." *English Journal,* 1989, 48(2), 30–34.

Hussey, C. "Groundhogs and Ducks: What Else Will the Poet Put in Her Doctorate?" *Journal of Critical Inquiry into Curriculum and Instruction,* 2004, 5(2), 21–25.

Kazemek, F. E., and Rigg, P. *Enriching Our Lives: Poetry Lessons for Adult Literacy Teachers and Tutors.* Newark, Del.: International Reading Association, 1995. (ED392051)

Orr, G. *Poetry as Survival.* Athens: University of Georgia Press, 2002.

Poindexter, C. C. "Research as Poetry: A Couple Experiences HIV." *Qualitative Inquiry,* 2002, 8(6), 707–714.

Richardson, L. "Poetics, Dramatics, and Transgressive Validity: The Case of the Skipped Line." *Sociological Quarterly,* 1993, 34(4), 695–710.

Sullivan, A. M. "The Necessity of Art: Three Found Poems from John Dewey's *Art as Experience.*" *Qualitative Studies in Education*, 2000a, *13*(3), 325–327.

Sullivan, A. M. "Notes from a Marine Biologist's Daughter: On the Art and Science of Attention." *Harvard Educational Review*, 2000b, *70*(2), 211–227.

Sullivan, A. M. "Poetry as Research: Development of Poetic Craft and the Relations of Craft and Utility." *Journal of Critical Inquiry into Curriculum and Instruction*, 2004, *5*(2), 34–37.

Tilden, F. *Interpreting Our Heritage.* Chapel Hill: University of North Carolina Press, 1977. (Originally published 1957)

Anne McCrary Sullivan is associate professor of Interdisciplinary Studies in Curriculum and Instruction at National-Louis University.

4

A composite technique blending photography and autobi-
ography, known as autophotography, was used to unleash
individual and group potential in a twelve-year participa-
tory community.

Autophotography in Adult Education: Building Creative Communities for Social Justice and Democratic Education

Keith B. Armstrong

In *Visual Pathways to the Inner Self* (Armstrong, 1996), I used a composite of autobiography, storytelling, and photography to investigate critical, reflective pedagogy in participatory adult education sites. Multicultural photographs depicting various social triggers helped the adults using the book reflect on the diverse forces that frame their lives. My follow-up book, *Visual Pathways of Diversity and Enlightenment: Critical Reflections for Transformation* (Armstrong, 2003), features autobiographies written by higher education students responding to photographs while in group discussion. As I wrote those books, I was not yet able to discuss the ongoing study of their theoretical basis, in what is coined "autophotography" (Larson and Brady, 2002). This chapter elucidates the context of those earlier works: a twelve-year study of the residential Goodman Oxford Institute for adults, which I incorporated in the 1990s and closed in 2003. I will describe the role of autophotography in building creative communities for the purpose of increasing social justice and democratic education.

A Phalanx of Social Change

Both autobiography and photography are remarkably powerful media because others often recognize some part of their own life experiences in what they see and read. Also, when people write about their own lives or photograph images personally relevant to their lives, they learn about themselves through the introspective processes required by the form. This process may help adult learners see principles of social justice and democracy more clearly, because life stories and photographs are a record of social interaction and the inevitable power relationships among the people interacting.

Autophotography is a process whereby in the beginning a person interprets the content of photographs (photographs he or she has taken or photographs the person is asked to critically reflect on) of both people and places that are actual or metaphoric examples of his or her life world. These critical reflections are then shared with a group of people trained to raise critical questions about what they see or sense in the photographs: "Does the photograph show that you are a part of the group, or apart from the group?" "Does the photograph remind you of your own uniqueness?" "Does the photograph remind you of how you feel at work?" Soon the participant begins his or her own critical reflection about the photographs, sharing with people in the group. This is usually a time of epiphany and awakening for the participants.

The process of learning leads eventually to recognizing the just and unjust covert forces that are the infrastructure of our life worlds (the sum of our experiences and responses to them). Here is where most adult educators' work begins. Many adult educators say that the hallmark of adult education is cultural transformation for developing the self (Rossiter, 2002); others say that learning theories become relevant for adults only through personal investigation and reflective writing (Larson and Brady, 2002). Still others say that adult education has from its inception believed in the need to focus on and expand democracy in society (Edelson, 1999). Together these notions suggest that adult education is ultimately about change, and that adult learners are the "protagonist[s] of their own transformation" (Daniels, 2003, p. 191).

Participatory adult educators, those using group synergy to both answer social questions and organize people into "protagonists," believe that group dynamics form a phalanx of social change. The phalanx of adult education, as various adult educators have shown, is often the efficacy of group creativity, although the participants may be "divided along ethnic, cultural, and political lines" (Daniels, 2003, p. 189). Yet difference empowers participatory groups as participants find venues for letting their unique knowledge be known. In groups where knowledge sharing and new knowledge acquisition are desired, some have employed autophotography to create highly reflective learning environments, not only to "trigger memories" or old knowledge but to make new meaning and inspire "new understandings of the self" (Taylor, 2002, p. 4).

Art, Democracy, Change, and Freedom

The Goodman Oxford Institute (GOI) was an adult education community committed to democratic inquiry for the purpose of generating diverse perspectives among its participants. My driving question in organizing the institute was, Can group creativity help individuals reflect on their lives, share those reflections in groups, and thus gain a greater sense of diversity and social justice from the process? To the affirmative, the GOI project demonstrated that a creative, stable, safe community can widen participants' understanding of diversity within themselves and expand their sense of social justice.

Today the adult education literature often incorporates and investigates diversity through transformational educational approaches for individual and group development and learning. Artistic initiatives have proven their efficacy for individual and group transformational education in many case studies as well. At the GOI, the transforming arts employed were photography and autobiography, although these methodologies were rarely used in participatory programs at the time (Taylor, 2002). The objective of these blended arts was to raise consciousness about social diversity and more generally social justice.

Social consciousness comprises two spaces of artistic potential: private and social. The intermingling of these two spaces, although not always harmonious, moves the learner toward grasping notions of self-understanding (private space) and how those notions lead to a desire to understand others (social space), promoting generative discussions about the nature of communities within society. Social consciousness raising is political in the sense that "political is not just about who gets what, but about who we become (through reasoning, evaluation—it is a transformative process of 'democratic talk')" (Schwartz, 1995, p. 14). Of course, democratic talk is not often a congenial experience; tension is a sine qua non of any democratic group discussion. On the basis of my experience at GOI and with other learning communities, I have found that without tension a democracy is neither evolutionary nor transformative. But when people listen to others' divergent opinions, they join in the process of "transforming action upon each other" (Hickling-Hudson, 1988, p. 23).

To summarize, art, democracy, change, and freedom of expression are central to any participatory adult learning community. Although individually they may be abstractions not fully attainable in society as most people know it, the constant reaching for them is in itself liberating. In her book *Art on My Mind* (1995), bell hooks affirms this notion: "Art was for me . . . a realm where every imposed boundary could be transgressed" (p. xi). At the GOI, photography and autobiography blended the private and public realms, individual experience and social life worlds, closely following Paulo Freire's use of photography and autobiography with oppressed people. Freire's technique was to capture everyday scenes in photographs; then ready participants were released to state their authentic lives and name their oppressions according to what the images triggered (cited in Shor, 1988).

The GOI began as a social action forum for local speakers. Within one year, it transformed into a residential program for people seeking a safe place where they could look introspectively at their lives; most participants had recently sustained a life-changing event. Although the mission was centered around the participatory community defining their own needs and therefore did not crystallize a specific mission statement, the initial advertisements welcomed people who did not want to live alone and who valued community interaction.

GOI's physical space was a remodeled neighborhood medical clinic and adjacent properties, housing approximately fifteen residents in private rooms. The social design for the GOI was, to a large extent, drawn from my experience and partnership with twenty individuals who built an intentional community and lodge in the wilderness of Canada. The five-year Canadian wilderness community helped me appreciate the nuances of community building, group dynamics, and creativity so integral to the success of the GOI. Although the GOI was not a wilderness location, the Canadian model factored strongly in developing the GOI's stable community life, which offered progressively stronger listening and participatory skills to empower participants to expand their boundaries of prior learning and patterns. The philosophy of the GOI was also Freirean in that the learning process was intensified by the creative experience occurring in participants' residence, not in a classroom or unfamiliar space. I found that adults who share diverse experiences and patterns in community are also more capable of hearing and supporting greater diversity in every aspect of their lives.

The use of reflective autophotography was closely directed in the first weeks of GOI's opening but quickly thereafter became an open-ended method that new residents were taught by those already using it. Specifically, counselors and the first wave of residents were asked to look at a set of photographs and talk about what they saw in the photograph. In a sense, this was a crash course in visual anthropology. Some people saw unpainted fences and bashed-in garbage cans; one participant said, "I see a shortage of money." Others would see in their picture a forest ranger, in full uniform, giving a group of kids a lecture about the contents of a book that was being held up, and the comment was made: "Kids are real quiet for that authority figure." I then talked about how successful they were at both decoding the photographs and demonstrating a sense of knowing about human conditions, because some part of the participants' life world was seen and identified in their comments about these photographs (in the first example, the resident understood what it was to have a shortage of money, and in the second example the resident understood posturing himself in silent respect for an authority figure). At this point, the residents were told they would now begin photographing and writing autobiographical pieces that critically decode visual representations of people, places, and things visually connected to where they live, play, work, and so on.

Out of Chaos, Transformation

Evolutionary adult learning continues throughout a person's life, "but in life stories you have to seek it between the lines" (Bateson, 2003, p. 2); between the lines the adult educator can also expect to encounter patterns of chaos experienced by many adult learners. Adult educators immersing themselves in the chaos of the adult learner for the sake of raising social consciousness should be prepared for the unknown. Karpiak (2000) asserts that "beyond the learners' comfort zone lie the true challenges to both the teacher and learner. This . . . is the space of mystery and surprise, possibly of chaos and even of transformation. This is the zone where issues of race, access, diversity and power reside, and where the responses become unpredictable and incalculable" (p. 38). For example, a resident at GOI who openly faced the chaos of her life as an immigrant agreed with Karpiak's assertion that "crossing cultures sparks thinking not only about immigration but about adaptation more generally" (p. 38). A man who had just divorced after acknowledging his gay sexual orientation also faced a kind of chaos, as Karpiak states: "Sexual orientation was to other males, learning to accept and live that orientation, and eventually relearning love, caring, and grieving in the world of AIDS" (p. 38).

The transitioning gay male took a series of photographs of himself in front of an open window with the wind blowing the sheer curtains. His autobiographic writing spoke of the new brightness of life, the refreshing air of hope, and the sadness that he could see slowly leaving his smile. Although positively experiencing transition in his life, this resident still felt the chaos characteristic of uncharted transitional territory. Astutely, Paul Edelson and Patricia Malone's work sheds light on how the adult educator must adapt to the multiplicity of chaos-generating experiences in today's learning environment: "The absence of a normative standard for continuing education gives this function great flexibility and strength. That is, within our individual contexts there is no reason not to try something new" (1999, p. 88). Photography and autobiography were the "something new" that offered staff and residents encouraging results, and the results helped them both remain open to the complexity of their individual transition process.

Some residents quickly appreciated the use of photography and autobiography; others were initially apprehensive. For example, residents in white-collar jobs or those from middle-income backgrounds rarely had difficulty with autophotography, but men from blue-collar environments often reported initial difficulty taking photographs, arguing that it was usually women's work to take pictures in their family. I could not fully understand these men's resistance until I read Ross Gibson's article "Where the Darkness Loiters" (2000), in which he compares human nature to a river where it meets the sea: "When a great river reaches the sea, it continues to behave like a river, maintaining its current and momentum through the engulfing water that will eventually subsume it. It agitates and influences long after it appears to have finished" (p. 251). Metaphorically, chaos-driven currents arose in some participants' photographic associations and personal storytelling, but they eventually accomplished autophotography.

Combining photography and autobiography gave the resident artists a tangible form in which to ground or contextualize experience. For most residents unfamiliar with self-reflection or perhaps verbalizing it, autophotography appeared to be an appealing method to begin the process. Dollinger (2001) describes the process of autophotography as "taking photos to answer the classic question; that is, the participant must think about the self as an object that is capable of being depicted through the external focus of the camera but, at the same time, with a goal of describing aspects of the inner self" (p. 72). Brookfield (1998) asserts that autobiography is a good lens for critical reflection because it "illuminates power dynamics and assumptions underlying experience" (p. 128). This type of illumination was uniquely realized by the older adult participants at the institute.

As early as 1933, Jung advocated introspection in the elderly because he believed introspection was crucial in old age for discovering meaning and achieving wholeness (Malde, 1988). Of the twenty-one residents of the GOI who were over sixty years of age, all mentioned feeling less whole, less important than when they were younger. They listed several ways in which their reduced importance was marked: people did not listen to what they had to say, did not respect their ability to perform known tasks, and disbelieved the difficulties they experienced in life. Adult educators confirm these experiences among the aging (Gold, 1982; Wolf, 1984). Mary Alice Wolf writes that older adults too often settle into passivity and "often do not want to speak; they are intimidated or they do not value their own abilities because society does not" (p. 1). At the GOI, these learners revitalized their identity through telling stories to staff and other participants.

Another area of transformation that occurred at the GOI is more difficult to explain fully. My day notes suggest that a few of the participants developed extraordinary gifts of heightened intuition. When these individuals began to demonstrate odd forms of intuition, the GOI community could not ignore them. One such case involved a young man, J.J., who alternated in his autophotography between demonstrating generosity and hatred, for no apparent reason. He was not even sure why. Because his unpredictable behavior was often noted in group discussions, J.J. asked the group if they could help him find the answer.

At the next group discussion, another resident told J.J. that he'd had a dream in which he was raped by a dozen tough kids. J.J. burst into tears, lashing out so violently that he ripped off my shirt sleeve. He shouted, "You aren't suppose to know these things—they should be buried, *forever!*" Later, J.J. revealed that he was placed in juvenile detention when he was ten for stealing a police car to drive it around the block. He was a small-town kid who didn't know how to defend himself, he said. At night, when the guards fell asleep, J.J. would be raped by a gang of older boys.

Unlike environments that are not purposely designed to heighten consciousness and intuitive understanding, the Freirean approach used at the GOI intended that engagement would influence the identity of participants, allowing them to move away from imposed identity toward an emergent identity of choice. Therefore, as heightened intuition occurred at the GOI, residents did not have to dissimulate or hide their development.

Another person, T.T., was a day participant brought to the GOI by his brother, who said T.T. had been labeled "mentally retarded" since grade school. T.T. carried an interesting cigar box full of cryptic messages on scraps of paper, saying such things as "Hate me, want out." Because the GOI had an open-door policy, T.T. was welcomed to participate a little in the beginning, and then he came every day for several months. At first, members of GOI noticed that his slurred speech and poor balance began to improve. When T.T. began to take photographs, we further discovered remarkable talent. He did not write anything in the beginning, but when he did it was what Karpiak said earlier: "Beyond comfort zones," in that "space of mystery and surprise [where] responses become unpredictable and incalculable" (2000, p. 38). T.T.'s psychiatrist and counselor watched his transformation with surprise, as T.T. taught himself to read and write at the college level; he published two articles and had photographs accepted into two galleries. Within twenty-four months, T.T. was a B+ student at the university. His parents often came to the GOI in tears of disbelief. I repeatedly explained that the adult educator merely provides a safe educational space where the forces that oppressed T.T.'s abilities were arrested, at least temporarily.

The accompanying photograph and autobiographic excerpt are examples of T.T.'s early work. Note how he simultaneously looks forward and backward in his life, capturing the complexity of a transitional place. Yet he is clearly rooted in where he is going and remorseful, not reminiscent, of a past filled with chaos and oppression:

> I know what it feels like to climb the pole and see the light on the other side of the fence. That's where I want to be. The barbed wire like addiction snags and holds me back. Life on the other side is beautiful, you can see in color. Even the fence is gold plated. The only way to get over the top is to start from the bottom and work your way up. If you happen to get cut by the wire on the way over the top, know that it took that much effort just to get where you are. You don't want to start from the bottom again.

T.T. is now a special education major, where he intends to use his rise to consciousness for those students looking for a way out of their head; when possible, he says, he will use autophotography. "It worked to save my life," he reported when last attending GOI.

Applications from the GOI Study to Other Contexts

The GOI was a modified participatory discovery group. The group made most of the decisions, including whether a resident showed signs of "getting into the culture" at GOI, a sign that an individual was authentically working at going beyond the mental or emotional obstacles he or she brought in. Such breakthroughs were so prized by the participants that the group as a whole would break into applause and cheers when participants shyly began reflecting on the meaning of their life world.

Once they began the process, many of GOI's residents commented that they were amazed they could produce something worthy of the group's interest; they were subsequently less fearful about doing it again, and they increasingly wanted their art to mean something.

Although academic commitments gradually caused me to close the Goodman Oxford Institute, its legacy may have value in other communities of learners. The knowledge gleaned from the helpful participants at the GOI is beginning to be used, with strong results, in programs conducted with at-risk young adults. Thus far, four one-semester pilot studies in charter high school classrooms have used versions of the GOI's autophotographic approach, and three nontraditional public high schools are awaiting grant funding to incorporate autophotography into their curricula.

Using Autophotography in an Urban, Nontraditional High School
I believed that high school students with high risk of dropping out, even in areas of high crime, poverty, and gang activity, could become more self-actualized through autophotography, as measured by more frequent completion of homework, more successful interaction with other students and staff (fewer reported fights and detentions), and graduation. The findings of the two-phase, four-classroom pilot study confirmed my belief.

The autophotography approach used with young adults in the urban high school (95 percent black and Latino students largely from poverty-level households) was identical to the one used at GOI, with the exception that travel opportunities were also integrated into the program. In one semester, twenty-one of the twenty-seven students traveled to San Diego to stay in a beach hotel and photograph a very unfamiliar landscape. The second phase and semester of the pilot study gave the high school participants a flight to Anaheim and a pass to Disneyland ("the happiest place on earth").

In both pilot studies, the students, now using digital and film cameras, began making a computer catalogue of their work, displaying it in the lobby of the school building and creating professional photographic shots of students outside the photography class, with the light and umbrella studio we designed. Their classmates' overwhelming reception of these individuals heightened and authenticated the importance of the work students did in the class, and it probably factored into the nearly immediate transformation of the students—even the autophotography students' parents started streaming into the school to make the same comment about the students' positive behavioral changes at home.

Using Autophotography in Nontraditional Adult College Programs
Using a similar approach with this second group, autophotography has the alchemic potential to motivate college students into new realms of personal and social engagement. The college students using autophotography from 2000 to 2003 that I spoke of earlier were adult undergraduate students in a nontraditional program in a private Midwestern university. The process of taking photographs and writing autobiographically about them drew the students close together. So closely were they drawn into communion that the first year's class was instrumental in designing and installing a new photography gallery to support their work, and the second year's class was bonded with an enthusiasm that motivated more than half of those who in the class to found a creative publishing corporation together. After raising the thousands of dollars necessary to begin their publishing house, all done within six months, they began and are running a success publishing house to promote creative works that express social and democratic reform efforts. They say of one of their books, *Open Genre* (Utsey, 2003):

> Found here is the delicate balance of editorial choice and authorial contribution, resulting from a year-long nationwide search. The works chosen for this anthology are a cornucopia of revitalized, hybrid, or a new perspective of artistic expression, each suggesting the genius of the unknown person behind the image or text. Each artist's short story, social commentary, or photograph has a special message to deliver—another part of the cosmic puzzle of why we live, who we are, what is beauty, and even what is evil. Although each piece may not speak directly to you, you may discover that each delivers an interesting message.

In this quotation, written by these adult students, they realize that everybody has some part of his or her life that "delivers an interesting message," as was discovered from autophotography. Further, these adult students realized that autophotography was the porthole that allowed them to be inspired by what appeared to be typical students—students they might not have truly known were it not for autophotography. As their mission continues to be one centered around giving others the right and opportunity to share their life discoveries, they fulfill much that they personally gained from autophotography: a forum for the lesser-known voices of society to be heard.

It is interesting to note that the urban high school students had little difficulty photographing and writing about their unique and complex life worlds, but such was not the case with the adult students in the affluent midwestern university. In both the high school and the university autophotography projects, students were given access to a learning program that began first with various professional photographers' work and their autobiographies, which the class studied, making connections between the two. For example, when the students read how the famous photographer Dorothea Lange struggled with her crippling leg condition and learned that Lange's own handicap encouraged people to trust her to photograph their lives in despair (and that her photographs often captured people in chaos and uncertainty), students understood how autophotography connects one's life to one's photos. For some students, making this connection is so profound that they want to immediately begin writing their own life story. But they have two learning stages they need to understand before moving forward. First, students were given lessons in camera use, especially the importance of close-ups and the power of shadows and negative or empty space, all helping the viewer study the data without unnecessary visual distraction—a distinction between art photographs and the typical snapshot that most people take.

Second, students were given autobiographic questions to answer, usually taken from one of several books on autobiography writing. These exercises were designed to warm them up to possible autobiographical points of interest; a great many students do not realize, at the start, that their lives can be interesting to anybody other than themselves. Although these same three steps in the autophotographic learning process were followed by the high school and the college-level students, the results were quite different.

The urban high school students' photography was expressive of dreams for their future, the gang graffiti of their neighborhood, their personal and familial melancholy or depression, and the incredible street smarts that composed their daily experience. Their autobiographies said the same, but more colorfully. One sixteen-year-old photographed the front door to her family's apartment, which the police had broken down the night before her report making. Her autobiography stated that her twelve-year-old sister was in therapy and the therapist mandated that the state provide her sister with a therapy dog for purposes of love and stability. Tragically, when the police mistook her family's apartment for the one upstairs during the prior night's drug bust, my student and her sister saw the police shoot and kill the therapy dog as they broke in. It had growled.

When stories of people's lives are delivered as art, they are more powerful (life-changing) for the presenter as much as for the listeners. The awe that settles into the minds and hearts of those present is transformative, and the bonding with the group is both emotional and solidarity producing.

Closing Thoughts

Introspection and the capacity to identify with the struggles of others are central to adult education. Similarly, autophotography is a pedagogy that draws into question many of the values and norms instilled early in an adult's life and potentially modifies them if they are shown to be oppressive. Additionally, establishment of a democratic, creative community forms a bridge for the adult to assess personal and societal spaces of democracy, or democratic values. Autophotography is therefore one method for exposing new groups of adults to the democratic values espoused in contemporary adult education literature. With the arrival of new groups of adult learners, we seasoned adult educators note that life is in flux or is dying; democratic change through creativity, even in subtle forms, can revitalize democratic inquiry in the educational domain. If adult educators look closely enough, it is apparent that everyone has a story that needs to be told and a vision that needs to be seen; if we recognize each voice, a more truly democratic and just society may emerge.

References

Armstrong, K. B. *Visual Pathways of the Inner Self.* De Kalb: LEPS (Northern Illinois University), 1996.

Armstrong, K. B. *Visual Pathways of Diversity and Enlightenment: Critical Reflections for Transformation.* De Kalb, Ill.: Educational Studies Press, 2003.

Bateson, M. D. "Lives of Learning." *Chronicle of Higher Education,* July 25, 2003, p. B5.

Brookfield, S. "Against Naïve Romanticism: From Celebration to the Critical Analysis of Experience." *Studies in Continuing Education,* 1998, *20*(2), 127–142.

Daniels, D. "Learning About Community Leadership: Fusing Methodology and Pedagogy to Learn About the Lives of Settlement Women." *Adult Education Quarterly,* 2003, *53*(3), 189–206.

Dollinger, S. J. "Religious Identity: An Autophotographic Study." *International Journal for the Psychology of Religion,* 2001, *11*(2), 71–92.

Edelson, P. J. "Enhancing Creativity in Adult and Continuing Education: Innovative Approaches, Methods, and Ideas." In P. J. Edelson and P. L. Malone (eds.), *Enhancing Creativity in Adult and Continuing Education: Innovative Approaches, Methods and Ideas.* New Directions for Adult and Continuing Education, no. 81. San Francisco: Jossey-Bass, 1999.

Edelson, P. J., and Malone, P. L. "New Vistas for Adult Education." In P. J. Edelson and P. L. Malone (eds.), *Enhancing Creativity in Adult and Continuing Education: Innovative Approaches, Methods and Ideas.* New Directions for Adult and Continuing Education, no. 81. San Francisco: Jossey-Bass, 1999.

Gibson, R. "Where the Darkness Loiters." *History of Photography,* 2000, *24*(3), 251–254.

Gold, S. "Educating the New Leisure Class: Teaching Humanities to the Elderly." *Lifelong Learning: The Adult Years,* 1982, *6*(1), 16–17.

Hickling-Hudson, A. "Toward Communication Praxis: Reflections on the Pedagogy of Paulo Freire and Educational Change in Grenada." *Journal of Education,* 1988, *170*(2), 9–38.

hooks, b. *Art on My Mind.* New York: New Press, 1995.

Karpiak, I. E. "Evolutionary Theory and the 'New Sciences': Rekindling Our Imagination for Transformation." *Studies in Continuing Education,* 2000, *22*(1), 29–44.

Larson, D., and Brady, E. M. "Learning Stories of Our Own." *Adult Learning,* 2002, *11*(4), 13–15.

Malde, S. "Guided Autobiography: A Counseling Tool for Older Adults." *Journal of Counseling and Development,* 1988, *66*(6), 290–293.

Rossiter, M. *Narrative and Stories in Adult Teaching and Learning.* Columbus, Ohio: ERIC Digest, 2002. (ED 473147)

Schwartz, J. *The Permanence of the Political: A Democratic Critique of the Radical Impulse to Transcend Political.* Princeton, N.J.: Princeton University, 1995.
Shor, I. "Working Hands and Critical Minds: A Paulo Freire Model for Job Training." *Journal of Education,* 1988, *170*(2), 102–121.
Taylor, E. W. "Studies in the Education of Adults." *Studies in the Education of Adults,* 2002, *34*(2). Retrieved Nov. 13, 2003 (http://search.epnet.com/direct.asp?an=8932192 &db=aph).
Utsey, T. (ed.). *Open Genre.* Chicago: Discovery Press, 2003.
Wolf, M. A. "Tapping the World of the Older Adult." Paper presented at the National Adult Education Conference, Louisville, Ky., Nov. 8, 1984. Retrieved July 14, 2004 ("http://proxy.uwlib.uwyo.edu/login?url").

Keith B. Armstrong is an associate professor in the department of Adult Learning and Technology at the University of Wyoming.

Transgressive and liberatory learning are explored through the creativity of popular theater as adult education when the freedom and power to imagine and raise awareness are placed in the interacting "bodymind" relationships of a group living with multiple psychiatric diagnoses.

Mental Illness Through Popular Theater: Performing (In)Sanely

Steven E. Noble

Imagine. Invisible but present. Performing but not seen. Ignored. Wanting to contribute. To be socially valued. Stigma. People running away screaming. They are scared in their ignorance. Not really of "the other" but in their imaginings of "it." Cloaked in silence, in shame. Oppression within stigma. Rituals become constructed through power relationships sequestering into ignorance the "not normal." When identity discussions arise, the boundary between visible and nonvisible difference is what is most often negotiated. (I use the term *nonvisible* to signify that which is visible but unseen by an observer who makes a choice not to see the markers of difference. *Nonvisible* can be distinguished from *invisible,* which relates to things that are not able to be seen whether one wishes to or not.) How—where—can transgressions from being less-than-human into fully free to be fully accepted occur? Within various social categories (dis/ability, sexuality, class, ethnicity, ex-prisoner, gender) are nuances of contrast—hiddenness that is often left unsaid, unheard, and unseen.

Within these realities is where much of my own research interest resides. Growing up poor, as the gay son of an immigrant mother in rural eastern Canada, now living in western Canada, I have become aware of many sources of invisibility that become repressed, ignored, and devalued. These attributes are screaming for expression and validation but seemingly cannot break through academic politeness to do so. With this background, I search for fellow travelers facing similar realities.

This chapter explores one sense of nonvisible difference: the realities of living with multiple psychiatric disorders. A recent Canadian book, *The Last Taboo* (Simmie and Nunes, 2001), highlights how this source of identity

New Directions for Adult and Continuing Education, no. 107, Fall 2005 © Wiley Periodicals, Inc.

diversity remains conceptualized by the mainstream. My writing describes the process and awareness that emerged during creation of a rural community performance depicting experiences of people living with mental disorders. Implications for adult education are considered.

The Claustrophobia of "Closets"

Nonvisible sources of identity diversity come with the protection of not being seen. Those people with markers of difference that highlight their uniqueness often have nowhere to hide. Within the closed-off and nonvisible worlds of psychiatric disability, the "mental closet" is where many remain. The mental closet parallels a metaphor used within queer theory. A closet can be defined as a small enclosed space; queer theory uses the word *closet* to describe something secret and unrevealed, as in one's sexual minority identity. *Mental closet*, then, refers to the secrecy of a mental disorder identity. These individuals are often entombed within powerful webbings of the mental health services industry. Well-meaning loved ones often reinforce this social exclusion by keeping psychiatrically diagnosed family members in institutions, thus limiting their participation in society. Caregivers often cajole that being isolated is "for the best." In doing so, they perpetuate the mainstream's systematic construction of mental disorder. Because of historical and continuing constructions of mental disabilities, individuals who identify with the mainstream interpret those with psychiatric conditions as dangerous, out of control, unpredictable, dirty, dumb, violent, or unsafe. Popular media representations help to perpetuate these views of mental disability by casting characters as criminals who are psychopaths or sociopaths.

When living within a "habitus," the realm of one's daily practice of living (Bourdieu, 1990), what is not often read is the construction of a closet. This notion of a closet also invokes the need to "come out" through a confession, and the twinned concept of "proof." Although the concept of the closet is usually associated with lesbigay individuals and queered lives, the mental closet also exists in very powerful ways. This concealment is less to protect the mental person than to maintain the cozy and safe boundaries of normal versus not normal, mainstream versus being on the margins. To come out, then, means to break through or transgress people's sense of expectations and ordered knownness of the world with regard to reason. At the same time, one discloses that one's self belongs to a class of people highly stigmatized and feared. Being rendered invisible implies a need to come out to others, which in reality is a lifetime of continual, repetitive, and embodied performances to render oneself visible, and knowable (Butler, 1990).

Another key aspect of being stowed away in a closet of invisibility is the idea of proof. Living within the effects of a psychiatric disorder, and wanting to disclose, evokes the notion of justification. There is the further burden of proof for the mentally ill individual to demonstrate or show the degree to which a person does not fit into normalcy. To be diagnosed with a mental disorder means a person has to "perform" one's body in a way that is interpreted by others, and that the behavior is often understood as being not normal. Within the world of mental disorder, those who distinguish between normality and abnormality are often laypeople, not versed in reading difference accurately.

There remains no conclusive evidence as to what causes disorders. The *DSM IV-TR* is a book of symptoms based upon clinical opinion and observed behavior, but it does not describe causes. The majority of medical professionals, who are white, male, straight, of upper-middle socioeconomic class, well educated, and urban, are the social elite who determine abnormality, as well as wellness and "fit" within the mainstream. This hegemony is underscored when a statistical breakdown of who becomes categorized as mentally ill is examined. Those who are nonwhite, female, lesbigay, from a lower class, or with less education are far more likely to be diagnosed as mentally disordered than those who more closely resemble the medical professionals responsible for the diagnosis. Does this mean that white, male, straight, upper-middle-class, well-educated, and urban people are more mentally healthy?

Some from within the ranks of psychiatry have problematized this perceptual gap between doctor and mental patient (Caplan, 1995; Kirk and Kutchins, 1988, 1992; Szasz, 1994). Authorities, both medical and social, become implicated in the construction of the mental closet. Because of some of these dynamics, the mental services industry was a target of the cast of learners living with mental disorders as they constructed a popular theater piece illustrating their lived lives with and within social margins.

Popular Theater Process and Performative Inquiry Lens

Popular theater has been around in various forms for hundreds of years. The intentional project of raising political consciousness, or Freirian (1996) conscientization, arose during the 1960s with Boal's efforts (1985) and the work of others (Barba, 1986, 1995; Barnet, 1987; Filewod, 1989; Grotowski, 1968; Kidd, 1980; Prentki and Selman, 2000) in the 1960s and 1970s, evoking the term "popular theater."

This form of educational and political theater broadly includes performances created by the people, for the people, with the people, about existential issues they face. Because the nature of the material that is drawn on is from immediate, concrete, lived realities, performance projects are carried out within informal community environments, away from elitist control and censure. The approach to creating performance is one of a socially systemic view of immediate issues. In this project, I embrace the enactivist and performative inquiry perspective. Where popular theater is a political education, performative inquiry (Fels, 1998, 2003; Fels and McGivern, 2002; Reid, 1996; Varela, Thompson, and Rosch, 1992) is a way to comprehend "interstanding" (Hocking, Haskell, and Linds, 2001, p. xxxiv) as knowledge unfolds from relationships within the popular process. It should be noted here that instead of understanding, a performative inquiry term is inter-standing, or knowledge acts that emerge among bodies. Performative inquiry is used here as a way to make sense of the linkages of insight that mark "paths by walking" (Fels, 2003, p. 239). Process and awareness emerge through unexpected twists and turns of the collective journey.

Knowledge within performative inquiry is reimagined as an act: to know is to do, to create, to be, become—and, I might add, to play. Through random and chance connections as bodies play and perform, twinklings and sparks of awareness burst quietly or brightly because "bodymemory" and "bodymind" (Hocking, Haskell, and Linds, 2001) contexts collide and "inter/re/act," opening up new and emergent insights.

This doctoral project of theater making ran from September 2002 to September 2003 in Duncan, British Columbia (pop. 4,500). A group of twenty-one adults ranging in age from twenty-seven to sixty-two came together to learn about theater and create a show uniquely their own. Six of the twenty-one were counselors and counseling students, and fifteen were clients of the mental health system. All were cast members. During the year of the project's life, eight of the fifteen mental health clients who came to check out our theater work left for various reasons: three because of timetable conflicts, one because he went back to using illegal sub-stances, three for health reasons, and one because he found employment. Of the four men and ten women who entered this ritual of popular theater to generate a place of power and safety—a tradition that was envisioned by popular adult educators including Freire (1995) and Freire and Faun-dez (1989)—seven clients performed alongside the six counselors and me in the eventual show. As a safety measure, counselors were fully involved cast members in the event that a client should require counseling assis-tance as the group explored challenging, existential, and emotional sto-ries and issues.

Creating a Performative Ritual of Popular Learning

As the group moved toward performance, Freire's cyclic process of decodi-fication and recodification and the evolution of group melding and effec-tiveness was drawn on in constructing a container for the group's work.

The first step was gaining access to a previously unknown community. To do this I moved to Duncan in the year prior to beginning my research. This relocation gave me a deeper sense of the town before gaining access to its citizens. To parachute in and immediately begin work only heightens outsider status, thereby maintaining the distance between his or her lack of local connection and that of the participants to one another. Once in, the playing began with weekly meetings. These meetings took place over the course of a year.

Each weekly meeting lasted about two and a half hours and comprised this ritual:

1. Meet, greet, and check in to determine where each participant's body-mind was each week, which served to move preoccupations from the outside world into the container conjured forth for the evening
2. A period of yoga exercises, working from lying on the floor to gradually standing and readiness to explore
3. A period of theater training, including lessons on voice, movement, dance, improvisation, and scene creation
4. A guided meditation and relaxation phase, moving individuals from the ritual space back into their broader lives

The broader yearlong theater-making journey included several periods, each lasting about two months. The first period was marked by a lot of game playing and group building. The second involved in-depth theater training. The third period involved discussion about lives lived through mental disorder and the creation of scenes and performance elements. The fourth period encompassed the rehearsals and performances of the play. The fifth involved the postproduction data gathering of cast and audience responses to the show. The sixth closed out the current cycle of popular theater while moving into social actions that arose as a result of the community performance, and the beginning of a new cycle of popular theater.

Once past the first two periods of group cohesion and theater "training," the rite of deconstructing members' marginalized worlds took place. Drawing upon the process of Freire (1996), the group entered into an initial stage of telling stories or codifying experiences. This was followed by verbally and performatively breaking down the issues into described rituals of power as they related to living with mental disorder, or a process of decodification. Once smaller parts of broader lives were teased apart, the group examined ways to reconfigure rituals of power into new rites of personal power for themselves. This bringing together in new ways is a means of codifying lives so that a greater sense of mastery of the performers' own habitus, or life practice, can be achieved. This recodification is presented to an audience as material for teaching and learning for the broader community about lives not often seen or known.

The show *Shaken: Not Disturbed . . . with a Twist!* was performed four times: once in a large poultry barn and three times at the local fringe festival. The postperformance stage was then an unpacking or decodification of meaning that was constructed by audiences so that the cast understood and interrogated the effects of their practice, amending methods and processes for the future, or a recodification of practice. This exercise of deconstruction and (re)construction is central to the work of popular education and theater. Insights that fell out of the group process interaction were caught through the lens of performative inquiry. It is to these that I turn next.

To Understand Oneself, Understand Others

This section explores a few of the key insights gained through the project. To draw upon the early overarching thought behind this chapter, the awareness of self comes through understanding others. To illustrate this, I explore three central sources of knowledge acts uncovered in this work: the cast as the insiders to the show; the audience as the outsiders or Others to the cast and as representatives of the mainstream; and me as the bridge between the first two, being both outside and inside the cast and community and yet a member of both.

The cast, usually under the powerful influences of medical practitioners and caregivers, found they had individual power. They discovered they can control their emotions rather than having their feelings take charge of their actions. One of the biggest successes for the cast was that they became aware they could commit to a large project and finish it. Living with mental disorder often leads to relatively low and fluctuating energy level and attention span. Working on something that lasted a year was unanimously cited as a significant mark of success. Through audience reactions and the support of other community members, they found that others valued their message. This translated into a new sense of self-worth and identity. Individuals found that they could be quite creative (previously thinking they did not have this ability at all) and found that the ability to express themselves included the ability to influence the mainstream.

Counselors in the group, being a subset of medical practitioners, found it difficult to let go of the process—to give leadership and control to mental health clients. This was difficult for a couple of people in the group. Throughout the process, they demanded that I take a highly directive role by laying out exactly what was to be covered in each session and describing what the results would look like before the group started. Not to know the outcomes in advance was scary and disorienting for the counselors, but predictable outcomes were not possible given the complex, chaotic, and ambiguous dynamic central to popular theater and performative inquiry.

Other counselors discovered the power of being flexible in a process as a way to have participants take the journey in directions not considered before: to go along with the group rather than lead. Counselors within the group learned to let go of process while discovering that flexibility is critical to learning. For everyone in the cast, the experience moved clients into what critical disability describes as "survivorship" and "mental pride."

The initial audience of 350 was made up of family members, friends, general public, and a sizeable portion of health care workers. Both the general public and the mental health workers held preconceptions about mental health clients that were based upon mass media portrayals. They commented that they were surprised to see mental health clients being capable of original creation and disciplined effort.

As a result of the performance, shifts in perception occurred for some spectators, which can be described by a metaphor: the play allowed them to see people with mental disorders in a complex, refracted light rather than the solid beam of stereotype. Related to this insight was an off-putting realization for spectators that they could not figure out which "players" had a mental disorder and which were the counselors. This was a disorienting and unnerving transgressive perception for many. Interestingly, a chant from the show was its overriding message:

We Are Mental: We Are the Same as You

I am I
> *you are you*
>> *the fear becomes*
>>> *I am you*
>>>> and you are me
>>>>> (Chant from *Shaken: Not Disturbed*)

My own interstanding includes the idea that nonvisible sources of self, that is, their mental disorder and my queer identity, hold similar notions of the world. Earlier in the chapter, I described the notion of closet and the need for proof, but stories described by members also included queer themes: passing, finding allies, guilt by association, flaunting, and "dangerous" sexualities. Risk ("infecting" others by passing on defective genes) coupled with a fear on the part of prospective mainstream mates that violence will be perpetrated by a lover with a mental disorder. This is reminiscent of the predominant perception that HIV infection is carried by gay men into the straight mainstream. Always it is the mainstream constructed as sacred, while Other is profane and infected.

As a result, I found the group's challenges in terms of the mainstream's responses to mentally ill people were similar to my own challenges as a gay man. I realized that the group looked to me as an informal role model rather than wanting me as a directive leader. Fostering flexibility and trust in learners to explore and be themselves was more important than having complete control over content or process. To be part of a contained learning environment that welcomes chaos and ambiguity is a lot more difficult and complex than teaching from books toward a predetermined result. This is because of its messiness, high-energy demands, spontaneous dynamics, and emotional nature (hooks, 1994). As a result, the process remains alive and rich. Reciprocal respect is far more powerful in achieving risky learning than if I, or anyone, is directive. To not trust and respect means that the risky and rich awareness is foreclosed. Letting go is critical for the group to learn in an animated manner in order to understand its own image.

{

52 ARTISTIC WAYS OF KNOWING

Implications for Adult Education

The implications for this kind of practice for adult education are many. Performative teaching informs teaching and learning relationships, adult education contexts, and knowledge creation processes. Power and control are fluid in popular theater so as to be most effective for knowledge construction acts. In many institutional sites of adult education, power and control reside with "experts" who predetermine process and outcomes in the absence of learners. In this popular theater context, outcomes were collectively set and cooperatively changed as required. To allow greater shared control within traditional institutional adult education, the same efficacy potentially exists and can be practiced. Forms of knowledge creation within a performative and popular educative experience include increased self-awareness, sense of identity, sense of autonomy, (re)gaining of one's voice, self-worth, collective knowledge creation and action, and ability of (and appreciation for) the power of the aesthetic process as a way of knowing one's world.

Downplaying individualistic and competitive learning creates room for everyone, regardless of background or skill level, to be included. The performative inquiry and popular theater approach is about the process of learning. The whole body in context is considered as it is caught in the action of understanding. This, in turn, is central to the performative project. The process is the outcome, rather than a prefabricated road to some externally fixed goal. How mental disorder is conceptualized and envisioned by the status quo is a larger metaphor for how the mainstream forcibly silences invisible forms of legitimate knowledge and identities into irrelevancy, while maintaining the status quo's own pathologies of ignorance.

This study also illuminates the power and control implications within the fields of adult teaching and counseling. The habitus of control is disturbed, for patients and learners alike, toward authorities and the difficulty in letting go of focusing power and control within predefined teaching and learning relationships. By disrupting, acts of knowledge move to being between or among knowing bodies rather than only within them.

In the postmodern era of prepackaged knowledge, projects such as this are created and negotiated through Foucauldian (Foucault, 1980) shared power relations, which may be more invisible but are often more accessible and powerful in a concrete way. Autonomy resides foremost within daily practice and multiple relationships rather than statically. In more structured adult education contexts, processes often become managed for efficiency rather than for learning. This performative experience opened up ritualistic aspects of education through learners intentionally constructing their own space, place, time, and interactions through reciprocal bodies interreacting in meaningful and empowering ways for them and their imaginative and creative potential.

References

Barba, E. Beyond the Floating Islands (trans. J. Barba, R. Fowler, J. C. Rodesch, and S. Shapiro). New York: PAJ, 1986.

Barba, E. *The Paper Canoe: A Guide to Theatre Anthropology*. New York: Routledge, 1995.

Barnet, D. "Out of the Collectives." *Canadian Theatre Review*, 1987, *53*, 5–6.

Boal, A. *Theatre of the Oppressed*. New York: Theatre Communications, 1985.

Bourdieu, P. *The Logic of Practice*. Stanford, Calif.: Stanford University Press, 1990.

Butler, J. *Gender Trouble: Feminism and the Subversion of Identity*. New York: Routledge, 1990.

Caplan, P. J. *They Say You're Crazy: How the World's Most Powerful Psychiatrists Decide Who's Normal*. Reading, Mass.: Addison-Wesley, 1995.

Fels, L. "In the Wind, Clothes Dance on a Line." *JCT: Journal of Curriculum Theory*, 1998, *14*(1), 27–36.

Fels, L. "Complexity, Teacher Education, and the Restless Jury: Pedagogical Moments of Performance." Proceedings of the Complexity Science and Educational Research Conference, Edmonton, Alberta, Oct. 2003.

Fels, L., and McGivern, L. "Intertextual Play Through Performative Inquiry: Intercultural Recognitions." In G. Braeurer (ed.), *Body and Language: Intercultural Learning Through Drama*. Westport, Conn.: Greenwood/Ablex, 2002.

Filewod, A. *Collective Encounters: Documentary Theatre in English Canada*. Toronto, Ontario: University of Toronto Press, 1989.

Foucault, M. *Power/Knowledge: Selected Interviews and Other Writings 1972–1977* (trans. C. Gordon, L. Marshall, J. Mepham, and K. Soper). New York: Pantheon, 1980.

Freire, P. "Pedagogy of the Oppressed." In S. B. Merriam (ed.), *Selected Writings on Philosophy and Adult Education* (2nd ed.). Malabar, Fla.: Krieger, 1995.

Freire, P. *Pedagogy of the Oppressed*. New York: Continuum, 1996.

Freire, P., and Faundez, A. *Learning to Question: A Pedagogy of Liberation*. New York: Continuum, 1989.

Grotowski, J. *Towards a Poor Theatre*. New York: Simon and Schuster, 1968.

Hocking, B., Haskell, J., and Linds, W. *Unfolding Bodymind: Exploring Possibility Through Education*. Brandon, Vt.: Foundation for Educational Renewal, 2001.

hooks, b. *Teaching to Transgress: Education as the Practice of Freedom*. New York: Routledge, 1994.

Kidd, R. "People's Theatre, Conscientization and Struggle." *Media Development*, 1980, *27*(3), 10–14.

Kirk, S., and Kutchins, H. "Deliberate Misdiagnosis in Mental Health Practice." *Social Service Review*, 1988, *62*, 225–237.

Kirk, S., and Kutchins, H. *The Selling of* DSM: *The Rhetoric of Science in Psychiatry*. New York: Aldine de Gruyter, 1992.

Prentki, T., and Selman, J. *Popular Theatre in Political Culture: Britain and Canada in Focus*. Bristol, UK: Intellect, 2000.

Reid, D. "Enactivism as Methodology." In L. Puig and A. Gutierrez (eds.), *Proceedings of the Twentieth Annual Conference of the International Group for the Psychology of Mathematics Education*, vol. 4. Valencia, Spain: IGPME, 1996.

Simmie, S., and Nunes, J. *The Last Taboo: A Survival Guide to Mental Health in Canada*. Toronto: McClelland and Stewart, 2001.

Szasz, T. *Cruel Compassion: Psychiatric Control of Society's Unwanted*. New York: Wiley, 1994.

Varela, F. J., Thompson, E., and Rosch, E. *The Embodied Mind: Cognitive Science and Human Experience*. Cambridge, Mass.: MIT Press, 1992.

Steven E. Noble is a doctoral candidate in Educational Studies at the University of British Columbia, a rural community researcher, and an instructor in performative research involving nonvisible identity difference.

6

Collaborative music making continues to be a powerful means of facilitating group knowledge construction and emancipatory learning in communities.

Music for Community Education and Emancipatory Learning

Kevin Olson

The history of adult education is embedded with community movements that were committed to acquisition of new knowledge, development of new skills, and empowerment of individuals and communities (Heaney, 1996). Leaders in many of these movements recognized the potential of using music to promote community solidarity, identity, and transformation. The potential of community building through music certainly caught the attention of several pioneers in the field of adult education (see, for example, Lindemann, 1926; Dewey, 1934; Horton, Kohl, and Kohl, 1990), and music making was an important component of such legendary adult education movements as the Chautauqua assemblies, workers' movements, the civil rights and feminist movements, and the Highlander Folk School, among others (Denisoff and Peterson, 1972; Denisoff, 1983; Glen, 1996; Simpson and Solomon, 1999). More common but less recognized is the adult education that occurs through the medium of music in a variety of formal and informal community settings across the world, in arenas as diverse as community choirs and bands, senior center and Elderhostel programs, ethnic celebrations and festivals, informal coffeehouse performances, private music instruction, garage bands, and religious ensembles, to name just a few. This chapter explores the distinguishing characteristics of community music; its rich historical traditions; and its potential to evoke personal transformation, collective consciousness, and social change. It further examines the challenges and rewards that community music makers face in creating an environment where emancipatory learning can take place.

In each context just mentioned, music can function as a medium through which adults evaluate and critique their life experiences and consciously determine new ways to view the world, a process explored in depth in Mezirow's theory on transformative learning (1991, 1978, 2000). Although the transformative process, according to Mezirow, must be self-initiated and often comes as a result of a disrupting dilemma in the individual's life, adult educators can facilitate transformative learning by creating an environment energized with discourse, in which participants feel trust, safety, and support (Mezirow, 2000; Brookfield, 1987). Many of the arenas of community music discussed later in this chapter exhibit these qualities and are an ideal opportunity for this type of learning.

Mezirow's theory has come under critique, specifically in its emphasis on rational approaches to the transformative learning process. New perspectives of transformative learning as an intuitive, creative, and emotional process are beginning to appear in adult education literature (Dirkx, 2001; Imel, 1998; Greene, 1995). Central to this new focus on intuition and emotion as a driving force in transformation is Boyd and Meyers' work in depth psychology, which draws on the "realm of interior experience, one constituent being the rational expressed through insights, judgments, and decisions, the other being the extrarational expressed through symbols, images, and feelings" (R. Boyd and Meyers, 1988, p. 275, cited in Imel, 1998, p. 1). Certainly, Boyd would recognize the music and other arts as a possible catalyst for external expression of these interior experiences.

Transformative learning does not necessarily imply external action, but emancipatory learning centers on freeing individuals from personal, institutional, or environmental forces that limit their options or control their lives (Apps, 1985; Imel, 1999). As with transformative learning, a major component of emancipatory learning centers on self-reflection and evaluation. However, the praxis of emancipatory learning carries with it the subsequent responsibility of recognizing one's connections with her or his community and then fulfilling requisite social responsibilities toward that community. Music has frequently aided in community efforts to promote emancipatory learning, and many programs continue to incorporate music for the purposes of critical reflection and collective action. In her dissertation, Gwendolyn Kaltoft (1990) found that musical interaction facilitated group trust, critical reflection, individuality of voice, individual and group identity, and dialogue at the Highlander Research and Education Center, the On-the-Line Music Collective, and the Augusta Heritage Center. Michael Rowland (1999) and Bernice Johnson Reagon (2001) noted similar learning processes occurring collectively in African American religious music. Music, in these and other environments, creates a space for a community to create identity, solidarity, and empowerment, providing a groundwork for imagining solutions to individual and group dilemmas.

Defining Community Music

Given the range of music-making activities mentioned earlier that could be categorized as "community music," it is difficult to apply specific characteristics and learning processes that apply to every situation. My own experience as a music educator inspired a recent study (Olson, 2003) in which I explored how music enhanced social learning, community building, and cross-cultural empathy among adults. The study was framed around the shared experiences of eight musicians involved in cultural education programs. This diverse group of educators used music in a variety of contexts, with wide-ranging objectives: some were involved with preserving cultural traditions within their community, others were more interested in sharing cultural traditions with audiences outside their community, and still others were interested in using music as a tool to create a democratic learning environment in a variety of disciplines. Through a series of interviews and observations, I found four themes to be the fundamental philosophies of this group.

Exploring Musical Ways of Knowing. First, participants agreed that music is more than a teaching "tool"; it is a way of knowing and understanding the self and one's relationship to the world. Music, to them, has the potential for "teaching" adults in four ways: fostering self-identity, physical or emotional therapy, awakening consciousness and spiritual connections that cannot be achieved otherwise, and forging connections to past experiences and cultural heritage. One participant explained how music created space for new knowledge this way: "People getting in touch with their inner self [sic], so they are able to see through the day-to-day monotony, what it means to live without really seeing the world. They appreciate it, because those beats, those dance movements will never be replicated again—those circumstances will never come back again. If I say, 'Well, I should have done that,' it doesn't matter. That performance is over."

Preserving Cultural Continuity Within Communities. Each participant in this study stressed the importance of community membership in her or his educational philosophy, although each defined the focused community using differing criteria for community construction. They recognized that music could assist in building group identity built on shared heritage and commitments, empowering individuals through active participation. Participants sought to create an arena of respect and tolerance, and many were focused on ensuring that cultural symbols such as music continue to survive against the onslaught of mainstream popular culture.

Building Cross-Cultural Empathy Through Music. Several participants in this study seemed most excited about the potential music has to create awareness, empathy, and interaction among individuals of disparate cultural, social, and religious backgrounds. Each saw music as a "window" into the life experience of others, which encouraged recognition, interaction, and eventually empathy among diverse groups of people. Several essential attributes to this process were identified: authenticity, contextual understanding, relativist interpretation, sensitivity, and respect. One participant involved in a multicultural musical ensemble explained how the process built bridges across social divides: "The love of music and love of sharing music and artistic expression brought us together. When a group like this is performing music of different cultures and presenting it to audiences of different cultures, there is a circle of life being formed where we feel each other culturally, give to each other emotionally, learn from one another by sharing familial backgrounds and experiences. If we tried to make a musical family tree, putting on it the names of those that were touched in some kind of way by music, it would be a never-ending task, but a wonderful one."

Promoting Collective Consciousness and Social Action Through Music. Participants stressed music's potential to inspire personal and social transformation by way of music, through recognizing individual and community commitments and connecting marginalized and oppressed individuals. Music created space that fostered engaged pedagogy, where hegemonic structures of power and positionality could be challenged and new solutions to individual and social dilemmas and injustices could be imagined. This space is described by country singer Rosanne Cash this way: "The essence of art is, if it works, it should reveal people to themselves. It shouldn't just tap into a vein that's already there and reflect back at them what they are. It should reveal something that's hidden to themselves. When that's working, it has power, power to heal and change" (J. Boyd, 1992, p. 131).

Despite the variety of arenas I have described, I observed that there are important attributes present in most community music environments that distinguish them from music making in formal or academic settings. Veblen and Olsson (2002) state that a fundamental quality of community music making is a flexibility of process and structure. I observed this flexibility manifested in membership that was often voluntary and accessible to anyone; the roles of members were fluid in these groups, as participants often moved freely from observer to active performer to leader within each arena. In contrast to the required training expected in professional ensembles and those in higher education, music proficiency was not a prerequisite for community music making in these contexts.

Community music makers recognize that each member brings a fresh perspective to the collective community, and the varied levels of expertise (or lack thereof) add richness to the process. This fluidity and accessibility gives members in a community music program a strong sense of identity, ownership, and responsibility for the welfare and direction of the entire group.

Quite often, community music makers consider the music-making process a means to an end. The goal of many community music programs is to recognize (and facilitate resolution of) the needs of the marginalized and disenfranchised members of a particular community, in an environment where emancipatory learning can take place. Community music that occurs in a youth detention center, prison, hospital, or senior center in particular often places the focus on personal and social progress over musical mastery. Cultural education, cross-cultural interaction, or intergenerational education can also be an end result of the community music-making endeavor. Powwows, cultural festivals, and folk music schools are just a few examples of arenas in which individuals can connect with their own cultural heritage or develop appreciation for and fluency in traditions of other communities. Facilitating the survival of cultural traditions or bringing to light the traditions of historically disenfranchised communities is a rallying cry for many community music programs.

Another difference between community music making and performance in a more formal musical setting is the emphasis on personal expression over technical mastery. Where most classical musicians have been trained to accept that there is one "correct" way to properly recreate each musical work, many community music makers delight in the flexible, creative process of improvisation and collaborative composition. Community music makers disregard a distinction between "high culture" and "low culture," finding value in folk and popular music—traditionally regarded in academia as inferior and unworthy of study. Eduard Lindemann challenged adult educators to champion the cause of folk art and cautioned against giving prescriptions by which all art was judged. By blurring the lines of high and low culture, adult educators could "aid greatly in the much-needed procedure of transforming a growing artistic snobbery into an indigenous folkexpression. . . . In short, adult education may justly be expected to do something toward democratizing art" (quoted in Brookfield, 1984, p. 520).

Historical Traditions of Community Music

Anthropologists have long wondered why music making is present in all known societies, given that it is not apparently necessary for a community's physical survival. Music has historically brought people together to worship, work, protest, dance, love, and relax. Some cultures have used music as protection against sickness, natural disaster, and other phenomena that cannot be explained by the community (Nettl, 1956).

Music has historically connected individuals in persecuted social and religious groups, giving strength and hope where it could be found nowhere else. Most music making in these communities has been social and inclusive in nature, and many of the conditions typical of community music already mentioned here were present in these circumstances. In the past century, several movements helped to preserve the rich tradition of community music making against an onslaught of contemporary pressures, notably a disconnection between the everyday experience and aesthetic experience of individuals, the rise of music in mass media, and a growing divide between classical and popular music traditions. In this technological age, community musicians are faced with a large number of individuals who experience music only as passive listeners and fail to see the relevance of the arts in their lives beyond mere entertainment and escape from reality.

Although community music making has existed for ages, centers dedicated to the philosophy of community music making are a relatively new phenomenon. The first centers in North America recognized as "community music schools" were the Hull House Music School in Chicago and the Third Street Music School Settlement in New York, both started in the late nineteenth century and modeled after settlement houses in Europe (Veblen and Olsson, 2002). These schools differed from existing music conservatories in that their focus was not on instruction of classical music performance but on cultural development, with the immigrant community and its children as a target audience. Lessons were made available to all, even if they could not afford tuition. Some of the ideals present in community music schools are found in a passage from a manual produced by the National Guild of Community Music Schools in 1957: "The Community Music School believes that music can be used a tool to aid in one's social development by serving as a beautiful and significant unifying factor in family life. By bringing together people from different ethnic, economic and intellectual groups to share a common experience, music can promote an understanding and appreciation for the spiritual values of all people, as it is practiced in these schools" (Egan, 1989, p. 91).

Following the success of the Hull House Music School, community music schools began to appear in other urban areas, such as Boston, New York, Philadelphia, and Baltimore; many continue running under these same philosophies today. The Web site of the National Guild of Community Schools of the Arts (http://www.nationalguild.org/) lists more than three hundred current institutions, serving more than half a million students.

In the early twentieth century, the Music Supervisors National Conference (now known as the Music Educators National Conference) noted a growing disinterest in American folk songs and work songs and began to actively promote community singing. The organization published several editions of folk songbooks, and "community sings" were organized nationwide. When World War I broke out, these community sings were an opportunity for communities to connect with their shared national heritage, and many traditional songs were sung at large war-band rallies. The community singing tradition also extended into the military, where more than thirty thousand personnel were trained to be song leaders for the troops (Mark, 1992).

After the war, community singing continued in movie theaters, and in factories, where workers would sing at noon and during rest periods. Even the Depression in the 1930s didn't stop community music making from taking place. In 1934, Peter Dykema (cited in Mark, 1992) wrote about hundreds of glee clubs from New York through Chicago that had performed at recent state "sings" and national conventions; he also reported vibrant activity in women's choruses, adult music appreciation classes, and national agencies committed to training community leaders in developing new music programs.

Music played a major role in boosting morale during World War II for troops abroad and on the home front. After the war, a variety of organizations committed to promoting music making in communities. For example, the Adult Education Association held sessions on community music at their 1955 meeting and subsequently formed a committee exploring the relationship between music and adult education (Kaplan, 1992).

Music in the 1960s fostered a large physical arena where members of social movements could define their space and identify with others of common beliefs. In movements promoting equality of race or gender, community singing again became a connective thread. Sanger (1996) writes, "Freedom songs became an important part of the . . . activists' attempts to construct a new sense of self. The songs offered a compelling means by which activists could communicate among themselves and disseminate a positive self-definition, and provide answers to questions about black identity and black relationships with one another and whites" (p. 8).

In these instances, community music was a vehicle through which a social movement could gain momentum through connecting masses with a common identity and a collective identification of injustice.

During the last part of the twentieth century, community choruses, bands, and symphonies flourished, thanks to an ever-increasing body of community members who have a musical background through school music programs. Local governments have recognized the benefits of these community ensembles. One notable example of this is the recent Iowa Band Law, which provided funds from state tax revenues to support local community bands (Mark, 1992). The growth of ethnic communities has spurred local leaders to recognize a growing need for a renewed connection to their heritage, especially among the younger members of the community. Mathews (2000) has researched the recent flourishing of contemporary Native American powwows, noting trends toward a younger community demographic.

Community music leaders are currently facing the challenge of inspiring active music making in a society where enjoying the arts is an increasingly passive process. There is a growing hegemonic assumption that arts are on a pedestal, to be enjoyed and performed only by the privileged elite with extensive music training. With the dominance of contemporary popular music on the radio and television, historical music traditions (both folk and classical) are becoming more remote from the everyday life of individuals. Attali (1985) identifies music as more than an object of study: a way of perceiving the world. Rarely, however, does it seem that people today associate their everyday experience with aesthetic experience; it is uncommon to hear an individual using music as a framework for personal reflection or critical analysis. Given this disassociation, it is no wonder that there is a growing call from government leaders to pull spending from music education programs in academia and in communities. It is important for political leaders to recognize that active music making in a community can effectively combat the increasing mechanization, isolation, and lack of creativity that has been a by-product of the technological advances in the past century.

Applications for Adult Educators and Music Educators

Despite the challenges mentioned earlier, community music continues to thrive, with ensembles, festivals, classes, and other programs catering to individuals from all walks of life. If amateur musicians look hard enough, they will see that there is usually a program close by that welcomes them with open arms, and if not then many will begin grassroots efforts to build a program. The struggle for many of these programs, however, is that they still fly under the radar of most music scholarship and dialogue.

Combining the resources and expertise of community and professional musicians can be mutually beneficial to both parties. I can think of several examples of a successful academic-community relationship at Elmhurst College, where I teach. The membership in our concert band is more than one hundred strong, and nearly half are members of the community, representing a variety of backgrounds and age groups (two members are over the age of ninety!). There is a combined college and community Choral Union and students are invited to the Elmhurst Symphony Orchestra, a community organization that is more than forty years old. We have a vibrant community preparatory program, teaching private and group musical instruction to children and adults of the community.

Although relationships of this kind certainly aren't unique to this school and admittedly have emerged out of necessity for a small, private liberal arts college, it does show how successful community efforts can be when combined with academic and professional resources. There is also still more work to be done. Music educators should look to see if any resources offered effectively in the community are redundant with the music programs in secondary and higher education. Are there additional opportunities to explore where community resources could enhance education in schools, and vice versa?

Like music educators, adult educators should become more aware of musical resources in their community and begin collaboration with community musicians and community music programs. Given the philosophies of community music leaders, the focus of this collaboration should be on collective music making, not the traditional guest-lecture-by-an-expert approach. The inclusive philosophies of community music should alleviate any fears about an educator's lack of musical expertise. Adult educators should look for opportunities to address cultural issues through music, allowing space for individuals to share their cultural traditions, as well developing stronger connections to the community through music making. There is also a need for adult educators to explore how adults can tie life experience to aesthetic experience, creating affective connections that cannot be expressed in other ways.

In his book *Art as Experience,* John Dewey (1934) wrote that the communicative arena of music could go beyond functioning as merely a vehicle for entertainment and aid in identifying connective elements within the community: "Works of art that are not remote from common life, that are widely enjoyed in a community, are signs of a collective life. But they are also marvelous aids in the creation of such a life. The remaking of the material of experience in the act of expression is not an isolated event confined to the artist and to a person here and there who happens to enjoy the work. In the degree in which art exercises its office, it is also a remaking of the experience of the community in the direction of greater order and community" (p. 81).

As adult educators look for new ways to encourage critical reflection, community identity, cross-cultural empathy, and social awareness and empowerment, joining forces with community music makers holds great promise in facilitating transformative and emancipatory learning in adults.

Once educators begin to think of music not as a curricular tool or gimmick but as a way of knowing, its true potential can be explored. Music's ability to bring people in touch with their emotions offers individuals the opportunity to affectively analyze and critique life experiences and begin to imagine ways to enact change. Music creates space for a community to create solidarity through cultural interaction and recognition of heritage. An empowered community can then begin to share its voices with others in musical dialogue, offering an opportunity for intercultural understanding and interaction. Music, in this sense, *is* adult education: an arena in which individuals and groups are actively engaged in transformation and empathy.

References

Apps, J. *Improving Practice in Adult Education.* San Francisco: Jossey-Bass, 1985.
Attali, J. *Noise: The Political Economy of Music.* Minneapolis: University of Minnesota Press, 1985.
Boyd, J. *Musicians in Tune: Seventy-Five Contemporary Musicians Discuss the Creative Process.* New York: Simon and Schuster, 1992.
Boyd, R., and Meyers, J. "Transformative Education." *International Journal of Lifelong Education,* 1988, 7, 261–284.
Brookfield, S. "The Meaning of Adult Education: The Contemporary Relevance of Eduard Lindemann." *Teachers College Record,* 1984, 85, 513–524.
Brookfield, S. *Developing Critical Thinkers: Challenging Adults to Explore Alternative Ways of Thinking and Acting.* San Francisco: Jossey-Bass, 1987.
Denisoff, R. *Sing a Song of Social Significance.* Bowling Green, Ohio: Bowling Green University Press, 1983.
Denisoff, R., and Peterson, R. *The Sounds of Social Change: Studies in Popular Culture.* New York: Rand McNally, 1972.
Dewey, J. *Art as Experience.* New York: Wideview/Pedigree Books, 1934.
Dirkx, J. "The Power of Feelings, Emotion, Imagination, and the Construction of Meaning in Adult Learning." In S. Merriam (ed.), *The New Update on Adult Learning Theory.* New Directions for Adult and Continuing Education, no. 89. San Francisco: Jossey-Bass, 2001.
Dykema, P. "Music in Community Life." In M. Mark (ed.), *The Music Educator and Community Music.* Reston, Va.: Music Educators National Conference, 1992.
Egan, R. *Music and the Arts in the Community: The Community Music School in America.* Metuchen, N.J.: Scarecrow Press, 1989.
Glen, J. *Highlander: No Ordinary School, 1932–1962.* Knoxville: University of Tennessee Press, 1996.
Greene, M. *Releasing the Imagination: Essays on Education, the Arts, and Social Change.* San Francisco: Jossey-Bass, 1995.
Heaney, T. "Adult Education for Social Change: From Center Stage to the Wings and

Back Again." Information Series no. 365. Columbus, Ohio: ERIC Clearinghouse on Adult, Career, and Vocational Education, Center on Education and Training for Employment, College of Education, Ohio State University, 1996.

Horton, M., Kohl, J., and Kohl, H. *The Long Haul: An Autobiography.* Garden City, N.Y.: Doubleday, 1990.

Imel, S. "Transformative Learning in Adulthood." Columbus, Ohio: ERIC Clearinghouse on Adult, Career, and Vocational Education, series no. 200, 1998.

Imel, S. "How Emancipatory Is Adult Learning?" Columbus, Ohio: ERIC Clearinghouse on Adult, Career, and Vocational Education, Myths and Realities, series no. 6, 1999.

Kaltoft, G. "Music and Emancipatory Learning in Three Community Education Programs." Dissertation Abstracts International, 51(07), 2239A (University Microfilms no. AAT95–34003), Columbia University, 1990.

Kaplan, M. "Community Music in an Earlier Time." In M. Mark (ed.), *The Music Educator and Community Music.* Reston, Va.: Music Educators National Conference, 1992.

Lindemann, E. *The Meaning of Adult Education.* New York: New Republic, 1926.

Mark, M. (ed.). The Music Educator and Community Music. Reston, Va.: Music Educators National Conference, 1992.

Mathews, L. "The Native American Powwow: A Contemporary Authentication of a Cultural Artifact." Unpublished doctoral dissertation, University of New Mexico, 2000.

Mezirow, J. "Perspective Transformation." *Adult Education,* 1978, *28,* 100–110.

Mezirow, J. *Transformative Dimensions of Adult Learning.* San Francisco: Jossey-Bass, 1991.

Mezirow, J. (ed.). *Learning as Transformation: Critical Perspectives on a Theory in Progress.* San Francisco: Jossey-Bass, 2000.

Nettl, B. *Music in Primitive Cultures.* Cambridge, Mass.: Harvard University Press, 1956.

Olson, K. "Bridge over Troubled Water: Exploring Music's Role in Building Communities of Adult Learners." Doctoral dissertation, National-Louis University, 2003.

Reagon, B. J. *If You Go, Don't Hinder Me: The African-American Sacred Song in Tradition.* Lincoln: University of Nebraska Press, 2001.

Rowland, M. "Missing the Beat: Adult Learning Through Religious Music in an African-American Church." Paper presented at the Adult Education Research Conference, De Kalb, Ill., May 1999.

Sanger, K. *When the Spirit Says Sing! The Role of Freedom Songs in the Civil Rights Movement.* New York: Garland, 1996.

Simpson, J., and Solomon, P. *Chautauqua: An American Utopia.* New York: Abrams, 1999.

Veblen, K., and Olsson, B. "Community Music: Toward an International Overview." In R. Colwell and C. Richardson (eds.), *The New Handbook of Research on Music Teaching and Learning.* New York: Oxford University Press, 2002.

Kevin Olson is assistant professor of music at Elmhurst College.

7

Community Performance Theater is a vehicle for creating collective knowledge based on oral history, opening dialogue in an urban setting, and paving the way for social change.

Scrap Mettle SOUL: Learning to Create Social Change at the Intersection of Differences Through Community Performance Theater

Bette Halperin Donoho

"When I first encountered Scrap Mettle SOUL [SMS]," said April, a participant,

> I was buried under a series of bad choices and bad luck. The only thing that prevented me from homelessness was my parents; they absolutely came through for me. I lost my job of seven years due to a bankruptcy. My about-to-be-ex-husband was a compulsive spender. He departed leaving me financially ruined. . . . SMS seemed safe; I finally felt I could breathe a little and dare to reach; I was almost pushed into reaching. Before I knew it there were stories, real stories and acting and the intensity that comes with being involved with creating a show. The process of doing the show brought me back to who I am.

This chapter describes how my participation in a community performance theater production gave me insight into the social aspects of experiential learning. Switching my role from college instructor to learner in a grassroots theater ensemble, I reflect on what ensemble members taught me about expressing life experience through the arts, creating collective knowledge, and paving the way for social change. In conclusion, I suggest approaches to learning for social change through artistic expression.

NEW DIRECTIONS FOR ADULT AND CONTINUING EDUCATION, no. 107, Fall 2005 © Wiley Periodicals, Inc.   65

Switching Roles: The Instructor Becomes the Learner

When I taught Perspectives on Prior Learning, a course in which adult students wrote essays seeking college credit for learning they gained from life experiences, I explained Kolb's theory of experiential learning (1984). I thought Kolb's theory helped students articulate their learning outcomes as they considered the four-part learning cycle: (1) concrete experience, (2) reflective observation, (3) abstract conceptualization, and (4) active experimentation. Believing I should practice what I teach, I decided to look for a concrete experience from which I could reflectively observe, and from which I could draw learning outcomes and conclusions (abstract conceptualization).

In switching roles from being the instructor to becoming a learner, I asked myself, *What do I want to learn?* Examining my life history led me to draw on past involvement in theater (high school drama teaching and directing) and community activism (American Association of University Women) to make the decision. As a researcher, I sought a grassroots community arts organization that would allow me to participate and observe, while conducting a case study of their performance process. For details about the role of a researcher in grassroots learning projects, see Donoho and Pfeiffer (2002).

Concrete Experience: Acting and Singing in a Community Performance Ensemble

As a white, Jewish, middle-aged, middle-class, suburban female, I wanted to experience working closely with people of other cultures and backgrounds. I joined the ensemble cast of an urban community play, *The Whole World Gets Well,* which was the spring 2002 production of a nonprofit theater company called Scrap Mettle SOUL. SMS was founded by Richard Geer in 1994, when SOUL (Stories of Urban Life), a teen-focused intergenerational project, merged with Scrap Mettle, a performance group including tenants of single-room housing in the Uptown area of Chicago. This group of people attracted me because of their diversity and their unique approach to the arts.

Among the ninety people who participated as cast members in *The Whole World Gets Well,* there were forty-three adults, five teenagers, and forty-two children. My study focused on the adult participants (twenty men and twenty-three women). I found myself among a diverse group, noting particular differences in performance background and expertise, economic circumstances, race, and age. Most were from the Edgewater or Uptown area of Chicago, but there were also people from other neighborhoods in the city. Class differences were evident; the cast included people who were homeless, the formerly homeless living in subsidized housing, middle-class, and affluent. For details of the case study, see Donoho (2004).

We rehearsed and performed in a park district building in Uptown, where I learned the mission of the group was to involve community members in an oral history-based performance process. When I joined the cast, two of the four steps in the process were already complete. First, members of Scrap Mettle SOUL had gone out into their community and gathered true stories. I saw video footage of story circles during which people would share bits of their oral history by telling stories of the obstacles they had overcome in their lives. The second phase of the process occurred when a professional playwright and a professional composer adapted these stories into the musical play, *The Whole World Gets Well*. I was an active participant in the third and fourth parts of the process: six weeks of workshops and rehearsals, and eight performances. Although I was an outsider commuting from the suburbs, ensemble members welcomed me to participate in this unique theater process. Community members gathered true stories from their own neighborhood and performed them for an audience of their neighbors, transforming urban oral history into "theater of, by, and for" their community (Geer, 1993).

At the time, I was working full time as an assessment counselor on a university campus. I commuted three hours (round trip) nightly on public transportation to attend two hours of rehearsal after an eight-hour workday. During a two-month period, I made the trip at least three times weekly in the beginning stages of rehearsal, and more frequently, including some Saturdays and Sundays, as it approached opening night.

In addition to the long commute, I had to overcome stage fright. Thankfully I was among friendly people, and most of the cast members were amateurs. Although I had some past experience as an amateur actress, it had been thirty years since I acted in a show. It was a humbling experience because I wondered if I could remember my lines under the pressure of performing for an audience, or if I could overcome my awkwardness, especially during scenes involving movement to music. I had no dance training or experience performing as a dancer.

On Reflection and Conceptualization

Reflection on the community performance process from the point of view of the learner led me to conceptualize experiential learning as a social process. Experiencing firsthand the humaneness and generosity of directors and choreographers who also served as instructors reaffirmed my resolve to meet students wherever they are in terms of expertise, before challenging them to reach for the next level. I was impressed with the respect that professionals, who directed the production, showed to the performers. Iega and Marion, choreographers from Deeply Rooted Productions, a Chicago-based, nonprofit dance and theater organization, made even the most physically awkward of us feel comfortable during a movement rehearsal. Iega accepted as well as challenged amateur performers. He reminded us that it was all right to make mistakes and stressed that we should not allow ourselves to lose concentration. Marion told us not to worry if we had two left feet, saying, "We will work with your two left feet." With a genuine smile on his face he presented dance as a natural, joyful activity and said, "You know how I made up these steps? I watch people walk." Then he demonstrated a dance walk, and patiently asked us to repeat the steps many times until we synchronized our rhythms.

I was glad that I shared the awkwardness of the learning process as well as the accomplishments involved in making true stories come alive through dialogue, song, and movement. As a researcher, it helped me earn the trust of ensemble members. Those who participated in the interviews and focus groups were willing to offer deeper self-disclosure than they would have given to a mere observer. Reflecting on the insights they shared, I arrived at three salient observations. First, the use of authentic stories as a basis for expression through theater arts fostered transformational learning. Second, the ensemble created a space where participants constructed new knowledge collectively, while engaging in musical theater. Third, the dedication of diverse individuals to a common musical theater project radiated energy for social change within the group, and out into the larger community.

Reflecting on Stories: Transformational Learning

Transformational learning occurs when learners reexamine their normal assumptions and realize new perspectives (Mezirow, 1991). There were two ways in which stories were the impetus for transformational learning. First, stories from the community that were adapted into the play provided a mirror in which ensemble members could examine their own lives. Second, as ensemble members socialized during the rehearsal process, they learned from each other as they created "ensemble stories" together.

"Treatment" was a scene in *The Whole World Gets Well* based on the story of a local woman who faced a crisis with an abscessed tooth because she had no insurance. The vignette showed her standing on long lines at the hospital, failing to get the care she needed at first. Finally, after a friend brought her to a clinic, she demanded care, making the point that human beings deserve proper treatment whether or not they have the financial means to pay for it. This story challenged the normal protocol of following bureaucratic procedures. Viewing the dramatization was like looking into a mirror in which an ensemble member saw her own struggle with the health care system and changed her perspective, helping her find the courage to make an appointment for treatment of a similar problem. In this way, a dramatized story from the larger community inspired transformational learning.

Ensemble members created their own stories and learned from them when they went out into the community together. For example, one evening after rehearsal, Wesley gave Sanford a ride home to the single room occupancy (SRO) building where he lived in the Uptown area of Chicago. Wesley, a successful advertising entrepreneur who lived in an upscale home, also in Uptown, had always assumed that "urban renewal" was good for the neighborhood. Developers in the area bought affordable housing units,

remodeled them, and sold them as condos for a profit, displacing the original occupants who could no longer afford them. Knowing Sanford and connecting him with the building where he lived changed Wesley's perspective.
He began to reexamine the concept of urban renewal and see it as gentrifi-
cation. Concluding that folks deserve to have affordable housing and should
not be forced out of their homes in the name of economic development was
transformational thinking for Wesley.

Reactions to stories in the show and stories unfolding in the community exemplified Kolb's theory (1984) that adults learn from reflecting
on their life experiences. Offering additional insight, Brooks (2000)
explains that people react to stories in cultural, emotional, and other ways.
Stories engage the heart and the spirit in addition to the mind. On multiple levels, people process stories for the critique (health care systems or
city housing regulations are bogged down in bureaucracy) and the moral
(all people should be treated with human decency). Consequently, stories
can be a rich resource, inspiring transformational learning and social construction of knowledge.

Reflecting on the Ensemble: Creating Collective Knowledge

The word *ensemble* meant in this instance both the collection of individuals
associated with the play as well as equitable distribution of power within
the collective. The ensemble was a community, gathering in one location
(community of place), and having common goals and values (community
of interest). In concurrence with St. Clair's definition of community (1998),
relationships among participants were especially important. Directors made
a point of acknowledging and valuing the contributions of all ensemble
members, making possible a feeling of inclusion rather than exclusion from
a "star system." In this atmosphere of acceptance, relationships of mutual
respect and trust flourished. One of the ensemble members described the
climate of the group as a "family type feeling." Like a close-knit family,
ensemble members created a reality among themselves that transcended the
exclusiveness of the larger community.

Coming from differing backgrounds could have divided people, causing factions and contention. However, thanks to the climate of inclusion,
those who had higher education socialized with people who had what Noble
called "differently acquired wisdom" (Noble, 1999, p. 2). Interacting with
each other within and outside the performance area meant there was a social
process of learning, which Vygotsky (in White, 2002) described as inter-
subjectivity. Social learning occurred when ensemble members solved problems collectively and constructed common knowledge. The ensemble
embodied Schwandt's belief that "knowledge and truth are created, not
discovered by [the] mind" (1998, p. 236). Knowledge and truth are more
than just cognitive creations authored by academics. Through community

performance, people from the neighborhood (not professors) constructed knowledge, and regular folks (not professional artists) created art.

Within the context of the community performance, people made meaning together, rather than individually as in the Kolb model (1984). They integrated perspectives, as in Mealman and Lawrence's model for collaborative inquiry (1998). This model uses a cooking metaphor, depicting a kettle fueled by attention to relationship, shared passion, and openness to divergent views. Ensemble members mixed experiences, dialogue, attentive listening, and reflection in the kettle, and collaborative knowledge emerged from the cooking process.

As an example, imagine about fifty people sitting down in their park district rehearsal room to a meal donated by members of their community. In an informal atmosphere, men and women of a variety of ages, races, ethnicities, and religious backgrounds helped themselves to food from a buffet and sat down in folding chairs to eat and converse with each other. They spoke about their life experiences, as well as their shared passion for the show.

In one of many conversations among diverse people, Kathleen listened carefully to someone who had life experiences quite different from her own. She opened her mind to the struggle of someone who did not have dental insurance, remembering expensive trips to the orthodontist when she was a child. Gaining a new perspective, Kathleen put aside her worries about paying her cable TV bill and was more concerned about giving an ensemble member a ride after rehearsal to make sure she arrived at the homeless shelter before it closed. Through their dialogue people from differing backgrounds created a social reality that overcame the oppressive divisions and exclusion occurring in their experience with the larger community. In this theater context, diverse people socially constructed the collective knowledge that they can respect and appreciate each other.

Ensemble members engaged in what Curry and Cunningham (2000) define as co-learning, by carefully honoring and appreciating each other's points of view rather than privileging one person's knowledge over another's. Just as in Curry and Cunningham's collaborative experience of documenting the cultural history of African American Pullman porters, Scrap Mettle SOUL paved the way for social change in their community by encouraging all participants to take equal responsibility for the project.

Reflecting on Community Performance: Paving the Way for Social Change

The people involved in *The Whole World Gets Well* exemplified what Noddings called an "ethic of caring" (1984, p. 79). This attitude of reaching out to others with respect and fairness became a self-fulfilling prophecy. The directors consistently showed patience and kindness to everyone in the ensemble and expected ensemble members to behave in a caring manner toward each other.

As leaders they demonstrated what Goleman (2002) described as emotional intelligence. Kyra felt the success of the show was due largely to directors allowing room for people to be self-organizing, giving them "breathing room" that motivated actors to feel a sense of ownership and responsibility. Eve described the sense of responsibility among ensemble members as "organic," explaining her perception that it came from within people, rather than as a result of someone telling them how to behave. In her words: "Somewhere in their hearts there was a little switch that turned on and said, 'I will take responsibility for the full group. . . .' This year I think that spirit was really alive, really intense, and I think there was a critical mass of people who felt that way, and it helped other people feel that way."

Commitment to each other and to the common project created interest in rather than fear of individual differences. This interest encouraged people to talk to each other and create connections. Sheared's concept of "polyrhythmic realities" (1999) highlights the complexity of bridging cultural differences. The metaphor suggests that people not only march to the beat of different drums but also have complicated perceptions based on lived experiences at the intersection of their race, gender, and class. How wonderful it would be if everyone realized that each person is multifaceted and therefore unique. Unfortunately, fear of others who appear to be different from ourselves often breeds prejudice and ethnocentrism, alienating people from one another. In the wake of September 11, 2001, Guy's contention (1999) that a culturally pluralistic society is still more of a dream than a reality especially rings true. Nevertheless, experiencing a community performance project among diverse individuals in an environment of inclusion, support, and safety renewed my faith that social change is possible from the grassroots level.

An appreciation of polyrhythmic realities created harmony in diversity. It established a meeting of minds and hearts that encouraged people to stretch their imagination. As Greene (1995) explains, "Aware then, on some level, of the integrity and the coherence of what may seem to us to be a totally alien world in the person of another, we are called upon to use our imaginations to enter into that world, to discover how it looks and feels from the vantage point of the person whose world it is" (p. 4).

Greene concludes that participating in artistic expression sharpens our senses and helps us release conventional thought in the process of imagining new possibilities. Participating in community performance taught me that expression through the arts also sharpens emotional intelligence and renews the spirit of people who care to work for social change.

Applications: Approaches to Learning for Social Change

Adult educators who wish to make a difference in the field cannot afford to direct programs or teach classes using the same methods year after year. It is important for academics to go out into the community and seek new concrete experience. It is not easy to walk in the shoes of the learner, but it is certainly worth the effort. Lifelong learning involves checking the ego at the door, and taking risks. To be authentic adult educators, we must be lifelong learners ourselves. We need to continue to learn from our students and encourage them to learn from each other. To be vital adult educators, we need to continuously seek new and engaging ways of opening lines of communication. Artistic activities such as storytelling, role playing, and incorporating music or dance can be especially engaging and offer stimulating opportunities for dialogue. When introducing artistic activities to adults in a college classroom, I have occasionally met with resistance. It helps to determine why students resist. If the problem is performance anxiety, creating a safe environment is essential. To establish a comfort level, I make two announcements: (1) there is no "wrong way" to perform a role play, and (2) there will be no grade assigned to the performance itself. However, I do evaluate papers that students write based on the role play. The paper provides evidence that a role-play exercise encourages students to think critically and learn from their experience.

Adult educators can also encourage students to present projects in artistic modes when they ask them to draw on their cultural history. For example, when I taught Multicultural Dimensions, a social science course focused on issues of cultural diversity, small groups each made a study of cultural backgrounds and presented their findings to the entire class. Presenters engaged their classmates in a livelier manner than if there had just been discussion about Mexican culture, for example, based on reading of a text. Seeing the ceremonial objects for *Dia de los Muertos* (Day of the Dead) and hearing their classmates tell the stories made the spirit of the tradition come alive. Thus experiential learning became a social process of sharing life experiences.

The nature of the case study in social science is that it yields specific evidence of possibilities rather than generalizable proof of social processes. However, the first step in stimulating social change is acknowledging that the possibility exists. Scrap Mettle SOUL's spring 2002 community performance process demonstrates innovative possibilities for adult education through theater arts.

References

Brooks, A. K. "Transformation." In E. F. Hayes, D. D. Flannery, and others (eds.), *Women as Learners: The Significance of Gender in Adult Learning.* San Francisco: Jossey-Bass, 2000.

Curry, R., and Cunningham, P. "Co-Learning in the Community." In M. J. Eisen and E. Tisdell (eds.), *Team Teaching and Learning.* New Directions for Adult and Continuing Education, no. 87. San Francisco: Jossey-Bass, 2000.

Donoho, B. H. "Scrap Mettle SOUL: Community Performance as a Catalyst for Adults Learning Through Grassroots Ensemble Theater." Unpublished critical engagement project (dissertation), National-Louis University, 2004.

Donoho, B. A., and Pfeiffer, B. A. "The Balancing Act: Researchers' Roles in Family and Community History Projects." Paper copresented at Midwest Research-to-Practice

Conference in Adult, Continuing, and Community Education, Northern Illinois University, De Kalb, Oct. 9, 2002.

Geer, R. O. "Of the People, by the People and for the People: The Field of Community Performance." *High Performance,* 1993, no. 64.

Goleman, D. *Primal Leadership: Realizing the Power of Emotional Intelligence.* Boston: Harvard Business School Press, 2002.

Greene, M. *Releasing the Imagination: Essays on Education, the Arts, and Social Change.* San Francisco: Jossey-Bass, 1995.

Guy, T. C. "Culture as a Context for Adult Education: The Need for Culturally Relevant Adult Education." In T. C. Guy (ed.), *Providing Culturally Relevant Adult Education: A Challenge for the Twenty-First Century.* New Directions for Adult and Continuing Education, no. 82. San Francisco: Jossey-Bass, 1999.

Kolb, D. A. *Experiential Learning: Experience as the Source of Learning and Development.* Upper Saddle River, N.J.: Prentice Hall, 1984.

Mealman, C., and Lawrence, R. L. "Co-Creating Knowledge: A Collaborative Inquiry into Collaborative Inquiry." Paper presented at the Seventeenth Annual Midwest Research-to-Practice Conference, Ball State University, Muncie, Ind., 1998.

Mezirow, J. *Transformative Dimensions of Adult Learning.* San Francisco: Jossey-Bass, 1991.

Noble, M. R. "Learning to Lead from the Middle: An Apprenticeship in Diversity." *Adult Learning,* 1999, *1,* 6–9.

Noddings, N. *Caring: A Feminine Approach to Ethics and Moral Education* (2nd ed.). Los Angeles: University of California Press, 1984.

St. Clair, R. "On the Commonplace: Reclaiming Community in Adult Education." *Adult Education Quarterly,* 1998, *49*(1), 5–14.

Schwandt, T. A. "Constructivist, Interpretivist, Approaches to Human Inquiry." In N. K. Denzin and Y. S. Lincoln (eds.), *The Landscape of Qualitative Research: Theories and Issues.* Thousand Oaks, Calif.: Sage, 1998.

Sheared, V. "Giving Voice: Inclusion of African American Students' Polyrhythmic Realities in Adult Basic Education." In T. C. Guy (ed.), *Providing Culturally Relevant Adult Education: A Challenge for the Twenty-First Century.* New Directions for Adult and Continuing Education, no. 82. San Francisco: Jossey-Bass, 1999.

White, S. R. "Organizational Model of a Constructivist Community: A Teilhardian Metaphor for Educators." *Journal of Educational Thought,* 2002, *36*(2), 111–128.

Bette Halperin Donoho is an adjunct faculty member at the College of DuPage.

8

The final chapter highlights five themes that thread through this volume: awareness of self, awareness of others, community building, social action, and art as a context for learning.

Weaving the Tapestry: Tying Themes and Threads Together

Randee Lipson Lawrence

The chapters in this volume explored artistic modes of teaching and learning, among them music, poetry, storytelling, photography, theater, and autobiographical writing. Learning groups spanned the range of new immigrants, adult graduate students, people experiencing life changes, and community groups in rural and urban settings in Canada and the United States. The settings and art forms vary, but many commonalities exist among the authors' writings. This final chapter synthesizes the major ideas brought forth in this volume and weaves the various themes together into a colorful tapestry. As in most tapestry work, the design as a whole has integrity while the distinct colors and patterns stand on their own merit.

All of the authors are artists who are passionate about their work. They are also adult educators whose subject matter or discipline is not art. (The one exception is Kevin Olson, who is a professor of music.) As each has attempted to infuse art into the curriculum, he or she realized that the arts still remain on the margin or fringe of what is considered mainstream education. This mindset is prevalent in elementary education, where funding cuts necessitate "art on a cart," and continues into adult and higher education, where art is considered an add-on to the "real" curriculum. These educators are mavericks in that they dare to try something different. They are persisting even in the face of initial resistance on the part of learners who, conditioned by prior schooling, are unfamiliar or uncomfortable with art making. All of these teachers/authors/artists have attempted to demystify this process by demonstrating how ordinary people can make and appreciate art and how art can be used as an educational tool. As Cassou and Cubley (1995) teach, if the fear of performance or concern about the quality of the product is removed, one is free to experience the process of creating art. It is within this process that learning occurs. In their own corner of the world, the authors are slowly moving the arts from the margin to the center through their actions.

The patterns in the tapestry depict the many values of artistic expression for the field of adult education. These values or benefits can be grouped into five major themes: awareness of self, awareness of others, community building, social action, and the arts as a context for learning.

Awareness of Self

According to Palmer (1998), self-knowledge is critical to effective teaching. To connect to one's learners in any meaningful way, one must first develop an awareness of self. Most of the authors agree that the arts can be a means for increasing this self-awareness. Through creating or interpreting art, we can go beneath the surface to see aspects of the self that were always present but veiled or hidden from view. As I discussed in Chapter One, art can be a way to tap into or access this deeper level of awareness. Anyone who has ever been moved by a provocative dramatic presentation, poem, dance, or painting knows this experience. The senses are heightened, emotions are stirred, and one might feel a tingling in the skin or a quickening of the heartbeat. Perhaps the memory of a particularly pleasurable or painful experience is recalled. In his discussion of autophotography in Chapter Four, Armstrong discusses the identification people make with art. People see aspects of themselves in the art of others. If art is shared and discussed in a group setting, the potential for self-awareness is even greater. Similarly, Donoho (Chapter Seven) found that hearing the stories of others helped people view their own lives from other perspectives. Armstrong believes art can be a means of making power relationships more visible. Noble's theater work (Chapter Five) intentionally makes the nonvisible visible. By deconstructing notions of mental illness and recodifying power relations, the self-image of the mentally ill participants shifted. The theater work helped them reclaim their personal power and self-mastery and see themselves as strong and capable individuals living with a disability.

Sullivan (Chapter Three) pointed out that writing poetry increases awareness of how one sees the world. Since poetry is a compressed form of writing (Sullivan uses the metaphor of packing the world into a tennis ball), one is constantly making choices of what to include and what to exclude. Ultimately, what is revealed is what is most important to the poet. This process is similar in other art forms as well. The painter decides which colors to use to convey a particular image, the musician which tones to use, and the actor which gestures to use to portray a particular feeling. When the artist steps back to reflect on why he or she made certain decisions and not others, much self-knowledge is revealed. Armstrong writes that photography and autobiography are naturally reflective or introspective processes.

People write about or take photos of what is personally meaningful or relevant in their lives. This process brings about a heightened sense of intuition and awareness, which in the case of Armstrong's population helped them shift from imposed identity to self-chosen identity.

Another form of self-awareness discussed by the chapter authors is awareness and connection to one's culture. The role of art in promoting cultural awareness was emphasized by hooks (1995) in what she called "visual politics." As an African American woman who once uncritically embraced the work of white male artists, she recognized the importance of becoming critically aware of the influence of race, class, and gender on works of art as a way of uncovering subjugated knowledge. In Chapter Six, Olson points out how music has historically been a means for connecting individuals from persecuted groups to instill ethnic pride. He refers to the freedom songs of slavery and the civil rights movement, which served as a way to unite people to raise awareness of and address cultural issues; he cites powwows and other cultural festivals as examples of people connecting to their heritage through music. Lems talked about the importance of cultural pride for her immigrant students in Chapter Two. Music is a means of affirming one's cultural roots and sharing one's home culture with those of different ethnicities.

Awareness of Others

Art in adult education contexts not only increases self-awareness but also deepens our awareness and knowledge of others. Art is a universal language that allows us to communicate with diverse groups of people and understand their perspectives. Art connects us to our environment and opens our eyes to expanded perceptions of reality.

In Chapter One, I talked about art as indigenous knowledge. Art is a way of knowing that can be shared by people who do not have a common a verbal language. Lems (Chapter Two) even went so far as to suggest that words are often an inadequate means of communication and that music can express what spoken language cannot.

Donoho (Chapter Seven) found that community performance was a way to connect individuals of different races and social classes. A climate of inclusion allowed the various knowledges and wisdom to be heard. Armstrong (Chapter Four) found people could identify with one another's struggles through making and sharing art. Communication around stories and photographs by the group participants raised consciousness about difference and increased understanding, which led to social justice.

Sullivan, Olson, and I all talked about how bringing in poetry, music, and visual art created by marginalized people or those not represented in the learning group helped the group members "see" from the vantage of the experience and heritage of others. Greene (1995) also used literature to help her students more directly connect to the experience of others.

In addition to increasing awareness of other human beings, art has the capacity to bring us closer to our surroundings. In Chapter Three, Sullivan discusses how, as a guide in Everglades National Park, she used poetry to help learners engage with the physical environment in order to "read the subtleties of the season." Similarly, Armstrong had people take photographs of their environment to see it more clearly.

Art can also provoke understanding, which can alter our perception of reality. In Noble's popular theater project (Chapter Five), unpacking the meaning of how mental illness was constructed by the performers and audience led to what Noble referred to as "interstanding" or emergent knowledge. Stereotypes were disrupted as new meanings of mental illness were constructed.

Community Building

The chapter authors agree that art is a way of building group identity and solidarity. The arts are often a catalyst for dialogue, which can lead to collective knowledge. In Chapter Six, Olson discusses how music has historically brought people together to work, worship, protest, dance, and simply enjoy time together. Although it may seem as if people are just gathering to have a good time, there is often an educative motive. He cites as an example "community music schools," which were designed primarily for cultural development of immigrant populations. In social movements, community singing is a common practice to connect people and imagine solutions to problems.

Olson, Noble, Donoho, and Armstrong all strongly emphasize the participatory nature of learning groups. When the decisions about art making are shared in a climate of mutual respect, members develop a sense of ownership and responsibility for the group. It is through this sense of group loyalty that strong communities are built and sustained. In Noble's theater group (Chapter Five), the members collectively determined the outcomes. The focus was on the process. The mentally ill actors not only developed community with one another but affected the wider community as the performance became a tool for teaching community members about a part of life not usually discussed. Donoho's experience with ensemble theater (Chapter Seven) was similar in that everyone in the group was equally responsible for the outcome. A comfortable and accepting environment was established where there were no experts and it was OK to make mistakes or not be perfect. For Armstrong (Chapter Four), creating a safe stable learning space was crucial to the group's solidarity and creative potential.

In all of the contexts exemplified in these chapters, art was created in a group setting. Sharing of art, whether individually or collaboratively created, was central to the learning process. The sharing of art often became a catalyst for dialogue. Donoho's performance group started with oral history or the sharing of stories. These stories generated much dialogue among the participants. Armstrong intentionally fostered dialogue as part of the learning process. In Chapter Four, he discusses how social interaction in the learning group mirrors the larger society, connecting this to promoting social justice. Photographs and personal stories were used as a stimulus for dialogue. Noble promoted dialogue about lived experience with mental illness through creating a performance. The world of the mentally ill was deconstructed and then reconstructed through a dialogue with the audience.

Participants in the learning groups created collective knowledge together. This knowledge was created though their art and dialogues with or about their art. This was knowledge that could not be expressed in any other way than through music, poetry, drama, or visual art. New meanings were created that served to unite and hold the community together.

Social Action

The role of the arts in social action is a theme threaded through this volume. Arts were shown as a means to recognize and address power issues, promote transformative and emancipatory learning, and bring about social change. Art can be the bridge that connects and balances power differentials and blurs the differences between healthy and unhealthy, teacher and learner, privileged and oppressed. In Noble's theater experiment (Chapter Five), counselors and clients were equal partners in all aspects of creating and producing the show. Audience members were unable to discern which were the people with mental disorders. In popular theater as in other forms of popular education, knowledge, power, and control are fluid, rather than fixed and determined by experts.

Olson (Chapter Six) also found this fluidity to be present in community music groups. Donoho (Chapter Seven) found ensemble theater to be a means for equalizing class differences. Group members included homeless people, affluent individuals, and everything in between. All had equal participation and power in decision making as they worked for the common goal of bringing their message to the community through art.

In Chapter Four, Armstrong, believing that difference empowers participatory learning groups, fostered transformation by structuring discussions to value diversity, giving all participants space to let their unique knowledge be heard. Noble also intentionally fostered transformation among the mentally ill participants as they "came out of the closet" about their disorder. This transformation extended to the health care workers and the community at large. People learned some truths about mental illness and what mentally ill individuals were capable of. The dramatization drove it home in a way that other forms of expression could not as the audience was able to observe real people up close. In Donoho's urban context, dramatizing real stories about community issues (in this case, health care) helped people see their own situations in a new and more hopeful way. People gained insight and encouragement to confront their issues. This is adult education at its best. For Olson, music was the medium for adults to consider and critique their experience and envision new ways of viewing the world. Acting upon these new insights for the good of the community promoted emancipatory learning.

The arts can be a catalyst for social change. In Chapter One, I cite popular theater and video production as a way of creating community awareness of issues and promoting dialogue aimed at changing society. Armstrong (Chapter Four) used participatory adult education methods, including photographs and stories by the participants, to promote dialogue and help people understand the principles of social justice. According to Noble (Chapter Five), "the process *is* the outcome." People learned about social change by participating in the artistic community. Olson, Donoho, and Armstrong share this view as well.

Art as a Context for Learning

Art making is a form of experiential learning that can be used to motivate learners in a variety of disciplines. As I have stated, the authors' objectives were not to teach art but to use art as a means to learn something else. The focus was on the process rather than the outcome. Lems (Chapter Two) found that music engages people. Most people enjoy some form of music. It relaxes, energizes, and opens them up to learning. Sullivan (Chapter Three) found the same is true for poetry, both writing poems and reading poems by others. There is probably no limit to the subject matter that can be taught through various art forms. Lems used music to promote language acquisition in nonnative English speakers. Sullivan described how she involved her graduate students in creating poems to understand and practice the skills involved in conducting action research (data gathering, analysis, and constructing meaning). In Chapter One, I described having students draw to recall the stages of adult development. Armstrong stated in Chapter Four that art gives people a tangible way to contextualize experience. The drawing activity was a way for people to get in touch with and contextualize learning from prior experience.

In Chapter Seven, Donoho described how theater allowed her to be a participant, not just an outside observer of the group. She experienced the theater process firsthand; felt the awkwardness of her body; and got to know, work with, and learn from a diverse group of people. Learning through art is always an experiential activity. Doing art, whether individually or collaboratively, through music, poetry, theater, photography, or storytelling, cannot help but result in learning.

Fringes on the Tapestry: Implications for Adult Education

This volume focused on the possibilities and richness of bringing the arts into the curriculum in both higher and community education. It is our hope though sharing our experiences with a wider audience that art will move from the fringes to the center of educational programs. As hooks (1995) says, we need to transgress boundaries and take risks with our programs, our learners, and ourselves as educators. To do so, we need to create learning spaces that are respectful, participatory, and collaborative, where people know they will not be judged. As educators of adults, we must honor multiple ways of knowing and consider alternative ways to promote knowledge construction and collective learning.

References

Cassou, M., and Cubley, S. *Life, Paint and Passion.* New York: Tarcher/Putnam, 1995.
Greene, M. *Releasing the Imagination.* San Francisco: Jossey-Bass, 1995.
hooks, b. *Art on My Mind.* New York: New Press, 1995.
Palmer, P. J. *The Courage to Teach.* San Francisco: Jossey-Bass, 1998.

Randee Lipson Lawrence is an associate professor in the department of Adult, Continuing, and Literacy Education at National-Louis University.

INDEX

Denisoff, R., 55
Dewey, J., 28, 30, 55, 62
"Differently acquired wisdom," 69
Dirkx, J. M., 6, 56
Donoho, B. H., 10, 65, 66, 73, 77, 78, 79
DSM IV-TR, 47
Duchamp, M., 7
Duncan Popular Theater project: implications for adult education by, 52; key insights gained during, 50–51; origins and planning for, 48–50
Dykema, P., 60

Edelson, P. J., 34, 37
Educating Rita (film), 7
Egan, R., 60
Eisner, E., 4, 5, 6, 7, 9, 30
ELLs (English language learners): expanding use of music with, 20; experimental research on music and, 14–15; music-based activities to use with, 13, 15–20
Elmhurst Symphony Orchestra, 62
English Through Music (UC Santa Barbara Extension course), 20
Ensemble (collective knowledge through), 69–70
Essentialist justification for art, 5
"Ethic of caring," 70
Evans, R., 19
Everglades National Park, 24–25, 78

Faundez, A., 48
Feldman, R., 30
Fels, L., 47
Filewod, A., 47
Foucault, M., 52
Found poetry, 28
Franklin, A., 19
Free-draw activities, 18–19
Free-write activities, 18–19
Freire, P., 10, 47, 48, 49
Friederici, A. D., 14

Gaugy, J.-C., 3
Geer, R. O., 66, 67
Gibson, R., 37
Gillan, J., 29
Gillan, M. M., 29
Glen, J., 55
GOI (Goodman Oxford Institute): applications to other contexts, 40; use of art, democracy, change, and freedom

in, 34–36; facilitating student life transformations, 36–40; origins and development of, 35–36; purpose of, 34–35; twelve-year study of, 33
Gold, S., 38
Goleman, D., 71
Gopen, G., 31
Gorrell, N., 28
Green, J. M., 14
Greene, M., 1, 4, 6, 7, 8, 9, 56, 71, 77
Grenough, M., 20
Grotowski, J., 47
Gunter, T. C., 14
Guy, T. C., 71

Halperin, B., 2
Haskell, J., 48
Heaney, T., 55
Hickling-Hudson, A., 35
Hidden knowledge, 7–8
Highlander Folk School, 55
Highlander Research and Education Center, 56
Hocking, B., 48
hooks, b., 35, 51, 77, 81
Horton, M., 55
Hull House Music School (Chicago), 60
Hussey, C., 30

"I Came to the Everglades with a Grief" (Sullivan), 29–30
Identity diversity. *See* Mental disorders
Iega (choreographer), 67
Imel, S., 56
Indigenous knowledge, 4–5, 77
Interpreting Our Heritage (Tilden), 25
"Interstanding," 78
Iowa Band Law, 61

J.J. (GOI student), 38
Journal of the Imagination in Language Learning, 20
Jung, C., 38

Kaltoft, G., 56
Kamler, B., 10
Kaplan, M., 60
Karpiak, I. E., 36, 37
Kathleen (SMS participant), 70
Kazemek, F. E., 28
Kidd, R., 47
Kirk, S., 47
Knowledge: accessing or uncovering

Vygotsky, L., 16, 69

Wesley (SMS participant), 68–69
"Where the Darkness Loiters" (Gibson),
  37
White, S. R., 69

"The Whole World Gets Well" (SMS
  production), 66–67, 68, 70
Williams, W. C., 31
Willis, P., 8
Wolf, M. A., 38
World music category, 5

Back Issue/Subscription Order Form

Copy or detach and send to:

Jossey-Bass, A Wiley Company, 989 Market Street, San Francisco CA 94103-1741

Call or fax toll-free: Phone 888-378-2537 6:30AM – 3PM PST; Fax 888-481-2665

Back Issues: Please send me the following issues at $29 each

(Important: please include series initials and issue number, such as ACE96.)

_____

_____

_____

$ _____   Total for single issues

$ _____   SHIPPING CHARGES: SURFACE   Domestic   Canadian

First Item $5.00 $6.00

Each Add'l Item $3.00 $1.50

For next-day and second-day delivery rates, call the number listed above.

Subscriptions: Please __start __renew my subscription to *New Directions for Adult and Continuing Education* for the year 2____ at the following rate:

U.S.	__Individual $80	__Institutional $170
Canada	__Individual $80	__Institutional $210
All Others	__Individual $104	__Institutional $244

For more information about online subscriptions visit
www.interscience.wiley.com

$ _____   Total single issues and subscriptions (Add appropriate sales tax for your state for single issue orders. No sales tax for U.S. subscriptions. Canadian residents, add GST for subscriptions and single issues.)

__Payment enclosed (U.S. check or money order only)

__VISA __MC __AmEx #_____ Exp. Date _____

Signature _____ Day Phone _____

__ Bill Me (U.S. institutional orders only. Purchase order required.)

Purchase order # _____

Federal Tax ID13559302   **GST 89102 8052**

Name _____

Address _____

_____

Phone _____ E-mail _____

For more information about Jossey-Bass, visit our Web site at **www.josseybass.com**

**NEW DIRECTIONS FOR
ADULT AND CONTINUING EDUCATION
IS NOW AVAILABLE ONLINE AT WILEY INTERSCIENCE**

What is Wiley InterScience?

Wiley InterScience is the dynamic online content service from John Wiley & Sons delivering the full text of over 300 leading scientific, technical, medical, and professional journals, plus major reference works, the acclaimed *Current Protocols* laboratory manuals, and even the full text of select Wiley print books online.

What are some special features of Wiley InterScience?

Wiley InterScience Alerts is a service that delivers table of contents via e-mail for any journal available on Wiley InterScience as soon as a new issue is published online.
Early View is Wiley's exclusive service presenting individual articles online as soon as they are ready, even before the release of the compiled print issue. These articles are complete, peer-reviewed, and citable.
CrossRef is the innovative multi-publisher reference linking system enabling readers to move seamlessly from a reference in a journal article to the cited publication, typically located on a different server and published by a different publisher.

How can I access Wiley InterScience?

Visit http://www.interscience.wiley.com

Guest Users can browse Wiley InterScience for unrestricted access to journal Tables of Contents and Article Abstracts, or use the powerful search engine.
Registered Users are provided with a *Personal Home Page* to store and manage customized alerts, searches, and links to favorite journals and articles. Additionally, Registered Users can view free Online Sample Issues and preview selected material from major reference works.
Licensed Customers are entitled to access full-text journal articles in PDF, with select journals also offering full-text HTML.

How do I become an Authorized User?

Authorized Users are individuals authorized by a paying Customer to have access to the journals in Wiley InterScience. For example, a university that subscribes to Wiley journals is considered to be the Customer. Faculty, staff and students authorized by the university to have access to those journals in Wiley InterScience are Authorized Users. Users should contact their Library for information on which Wiley journals they have access to in Wiley InterScience.

ASK YOUR INSTITUTION ABOUT WILEY INTERSCIENCE TODAY!